MORE PRAISE FOR *PASSION BRANDS*

"Kate Newlin has done it again. Her latest book demonstrates the power of passion brands to spark our interests, inspire our purchases, and even question those who don't agree. After all, passion brands are more reliable, always meet our expectations, and never disagree. This is a must read for brand builders and brand buyers alike."
   —Daryl Brewster, retired president and CEO of
      Krispy Kreme, and former president, Nabisco Brands

"While many brands are drowning in a sea of sameness, those that instill a strong emotional bond with their clientele clearly stand out among the rest. *Passion Brands* explores the concept of intense brand loyalty and fascinatingly explains the seven stages of passion creation, making it a must read for executives looking for a competitive advantage."
   —Shari Hershon, design consultant and former
      senior vice president of design for Ann Taylor LOFT

"Kate Newlin has raised a timely and fascinating issue that few of us can even articulate: how one's passion for a brand becomes a key personality trait that can alter personal relationships for better or worse."
   —Robert Lee Morris, renowned jewelry designer
      and author of *The Power of Jewelry*

Passion
BRANDS

Kate Newlin

Passion
BRANDS

Why Some Brands Are

JUST GOTTA HAVE,

DRIVE ALL NIGHT FOR,

and **TELL ALL YOUR**

FRIENDS ABOUT

Prometheus Books

59 John Glenn Drive
Amherst, New York 14228–2119

Published 2009 by Prometheus Books

Inquiries should be addressed to
Prometheus Books
59 John Glenn Drive
Amherst, New York 14228–2119
VOICE: 716–691–0133, ext. 210
FAX: 716–691–0137
WWW.PROMETHEUSBOOKS.COM

13 12 11 10 09   5 4 3 2 1

Library of Congress Cataloging-in-Publication Data

Newlin, Kate.
    Passion brands : why some brands are just gotta have, drive all night for, and tell all your friends about / by Kate Newlin.
        p. cm.
    Includes index.
    ISBN 978–1–59102–687–7 (hardcover : alk. paper)
    1. Brand name products. 2. Consumers—Attitudes. 3. Customer loyalty.
4. Branding (Marketing)

HD69.B7 N42 2009
658.8/27 22

                                                                2008049550

Printed in the United States of America on acid-free paper

*For Mattie, my daughter and
the most passionate person I know*

CONTENTS

FOREWORD

Mark DiMassimo

If you want to get anyone to do anything, you are in the business of arousing passion.

I say this based not just on a more than two-decade career being remarkably effective at getting people to do things, but also based on science. Behavioral economics is a relatively new discipline that explores the causes of economic decision making. This has already led to a lot of fascinating science and to some terrific books, such as *Freakonomics* by Steven D. Levitt and Stephen J. Dubner and Dan Arielly's *Predictably Irrational*.

One of Arielly's conclusions: People not only behave differently when their passions are aroused; they are almost like *different people*. This makes it nearly impossible to predict how we will behave when passion turns us into that other person. One thing is clear: whatever it is that excites our passion, it is passion itself that encourages us to take action—stronger action and more often than when we're in thrall to our more rational temperament.

So imagine the advantages enjoyed by a brand that truly excites enduring passion in its customers. It is as if these brands compete *in a different marketplace*. The rules that apply to competitors don't hold for these brands. People who might think they want to make cold, rational choices about which PC to buy and what to pay are suddenly besotted by their Apple Mac purchase.

Why don't more businesses do what it takes to become passion brands? Why don't they prioritize it? Is it because, as business professionals, they spend so much time trying not to follow passion over the cliff? Is it because they feel they must be rational and therefore think that everyone really does make rational decisions? Is it because they know deep down that passion is very strong stuff and that it will require their engagement on a much higher level? Or are there still businesspeople out there who believe that the old "rational actor" economic model they learned in school still stands, that all this talk of passion is just "soft stuff" having little effect on hard business realities?

If so, Kate Newlin will disabuse them of that notion once and for all, and they'll be a lot more successful for it. I believe she's found the seven accelerators of creating passion brands and I believe we can create considerable market value by following them, being engaged by them, and challenging ourselves to bring our own passion to the process.

In my career, I've seen the huge business advantages that make passion brands into much better businesses. I've seen it with entrepreneurial companies that played David with passion as their slingshots swiftly took down massive Goliaths. I've seen the higher margins, longer and more-profitable relationships, market permission to succeed with line extensions, massive reputational forgiveness, higher, more stable market caps, and even the ability to rise like a phoenix from the ashes of huge business miscalculations.

I've actually seen people—customers, employees, and advocates all—willing, even anxious, to sacrifice and suffer for the object of their passion.

Passion is an intense experience, full of powerful emotions, both positive and negative. The difference between the popular conception of passion and the real thing is akin to the difference between porn and true love. There are, of course, similarities at the level of appearance, but that's about as far as it goes.

Passion brands are the extreme refutation of this "porn" concept. By the act of choice, we connect. Through our enjoyment we come to love. Through identification we develop passion. Rather than seeing these objects as our products, we see them as ourselves. No wonder we are so hurt when we find that people we like or love don't see them the same way.

I have been fortunate to spend the better part of my now more than twenty-year career working on passion brands. They are different, and the people behind them are different, too.

I've had the privilege to work, at different times of course, on both the Apple and the Gateway brands. In 1998 Gateway was neck and neck with Dell, both with $8 billion in sales, and Apple was hurting, having dropped below the $2-billion revenue mark that year. The fortunes of these two companies have overwhelmingly reversed, and the difference is not just in the passion of the founders, but in the passion of the users of these brands.

Ted Waitt, the founder of Gateway, the visionary who put the cow spots on the boxes, had built the closest thing to a passion brand in personal computers. People engaged with its imaginative presentation of itself, its loopy farmland identity, and its direct-to-consumer business model. Gateway vanquished scores of other direct-to-consumer PC clone companies and maintained pace with the much more MBA'ed Dell.

Then Waitt allowed the passion to drain out of Gateway; he turned the management of the company over to hard, rational business types, and then had to witness his passion die a slow death. Over the next decade the value of the company declined to the point where it was sold to Acer for well under a billion dollars. Somewhere in there, among the ashes, the embers of a passion brand still glow, I think. It is with an irrational level of sadness that I admit to pessimism about someone blowing those embers back to life anytime soon. But that is what Steve Jobs was able to do with Apple, wasn't it?

"Do you want to sell sugar water the rest of your life or do you want to change the world?" he asked Pepsi executive John Sculley, in order to lure him to Silicon Valley. Not long afterward, the maestro of passion was out and the former sugar water peddler was in charge at Apple. Apple slid into near irrelevance. Yet the passion burned brightly among the creative set and the growing subculture of graphic artists, designers, and increasingly computer-enabled entertainment and creative communications professionals. They kept the flame alive and when Jobs returned, the pent-up passion was there to greet him and to support his plans for resurrection.

People think Jobs is different, a unique case. Of course he is. But the principles and advantages of the passion brand are much more broadly applicable than is commonly imagined. Whether consumer product, service, or business to business, there is simply no good reason not to aim for passion brand status. If we reach for the stars, at least we won't come up with a handful of dirt.

Let the idea of the passion brand be your guiding star and let Kate Newlin, just as she has done for many of the most successful marketers of our time, be your guide.

Mark DiMassimo
CEO, chief brand officer
DiMassimo Goldstein (DIGO)
New York City

Part One

SEVEN ACCELERATORS OF PASSION BRANDING

Chapter 1

THE BRANDS WE LOVE

The Scene: Me at home with my daughter, Mattie, cooking dinner for some friends.

The Discussion: I begin bragging about the great service Fresh Direct provides. It's only available here in New York City; other cities may have other versions of it. The basic promise is exceptionally fresh food, delivered directly to me. Never, ever having to go to the grocery store. No running out of crucial ingredients. As Fresh Direct ads say, "Our food is fresh. Our customers are spoiled."

The Reaction: My guests begin to question my enthusiasm for the company. Isn't it too expensive? What about all the boxes the food arrives in? What happens to those? Isn't it environmentally irresponsible to have those trucks running all over the city instead of just walking to the store? What about the delivery fees? Isn't it a pain to have to be home to receive deliveries?

I found I was dumbstruck by their reactions and I was taking it personally. I had to admit I was wounded by their comments—to my mind, their *quibbling*.

Indeed, in order to participate in the Fresh Direct experience, you must order your groceries online and specify a delivery time within a two-hour window when you'll be home to receive them.

But, I responded, surely you know when you're going to be home tomorrow. And even more surely, watching the news or playing Hearts with your children is eminently more engaging than going into a New York City grocery store and trying to get eye contact with a bored (or furious) employee in order to determine the difference between two cuts of lamb, only to then have to bag the stuff yourself and schlep it home. Surely they weren't seriously suggesting that it's more fun or rewarding or interesting to trek through the gritty aisles with a wobbly-wheeled cart and a tired four-year-old.

My friends' response *was* exasperating me—but why? They are terrific people. We have much in common, including children who adore each other. We are members of the same church. We share a worldview. We have wonderful evenings together. But something was going south. I found myself looking at them in a different way, as if they'd made some irredeemable social faux pas.

Actually, they had, in a postmodern marketing sort of way. They did not love "my" brand the way I do. How can this be? How can I have a relationship with a brand that is actually stronger than my relationship with these good and trusted friends?

The Epiphany: That's when it hit me. The idea of the passion brand, a brand you recommend to friends wholeheartedly, even evangelically—so much so that, if they don't embrace it as vigorously as you do, you perceive a cloud over *their* heads, blocking the sunshine of the brand. Yes, of course, momentarily. The cloud moves on and the friendship remains. But still. What is going on?

* * *

There are brands we dislike. There are brands we tolerate or simply put up with, but to which we have no real connection. There are brands we like, even love. Some we grew up with and feel as though they are part of our history.

And then again there are brands of an entirely different stripe: brands we are *passionate* about. A brand we will search for, accepting no substitute. Not just walk across the street to find, but across town, driving far *and driven to great lengths* just to have *It*. These are brands that will help establish friendships: "Anyone who loves *Law & Order* reruns as much as I do must be my kind of person." Think about the love affair women (in particular) had with *Sex in the City* on HBO: The get-togethers to view, water cooler discussions the mornings after, parties to say farewell, field trips to shop the stores and drink the cocktails, the collector DVD editions, those seemingly endless cable reruns and reunion expeditions to view the movie the moment it opened. All these are the stuff of passion. For those who missed the wave, it just seemed like one endless chick flick. There was little room in between. It was either a consuming, viewing passion or a channel-surfing shrug. In either case, there was a brand (or anti-brand) bonding that took place. You cared about Carrie, or you didn't, but in either case your reaction to the phenomenon spoke cultural volumes about you and your values, your taste, your sense of humor. The show's brand served as a magnet to attract or repel.

These are the brands that have the power to make some friendships tremble a bit, as one friend described it: "She recommended a certain movie to me and I went to see it on the strength of her saying it was fabulous. I couldn't imagine what she was thinking—or what she thought of me! It put her in an entirely new and I have to say unflattering light."

These are the brands that change lifelong behavior—grocery shopping, for example. My passion brand would cause me to inquire before considering a move to a new, otherwise more convenient neighborhood: "Does Fresh Direct deliver here?"

A brand litmus test, for instance. Colgate or Crest? Poet Julie Sheehan told me that somehow she'd acquired a tube of Colgate and was clueless how to get rid of it. It seemed nuts to just toss it out, but then again, brush her teeth with it? I told her that in the army we used it to polish brass, which seemed as good a task as any, at least for Crest loyalists.

In other words, a passion brand is a brand you form such a personal attachment to that it becomes an indelible aspect of your identity, even when no one is looking. Passion brands cause you to reevaluate your habits, your behaviors, your understanding of what makes a good apartment location, and your relationships with others—friends, colleagues, and family.

If Webster were writing the definition, it might go something like this:

> **passion brand** ('pash ən brand), n. 1. a product so extravagantly lovable that its advocates must spontaneously speak of it, sharing their ardor for it with friends, family, and colleagues, requiring them to love it too. 2. a product that creates such personal enthusiasm that purchasers badge themselves with it through conversation, apparel, continuous repeat purchase. 3. a brand built day by day with the deep love and joyous advocacy of its consumers.

A passion brand is something far beyond a brand that enjoys positive word of mouth, which, after all, has been around since the snake told Eve about the joys of the apple. A passion brand is one with which we have a relationship more powerful than those we have with many human beings. That's right: We're relating to a thing, a brand, a totem more passionately than we do to some of the people in our lives.

A phenomenon like this cries out to be explored, and so I did. I found that the process through which a brand ignites passion in its users goes beyond the social, cultural, and intellectual intrigue of asking, *"What's going on here?"* although that is a fascinating topic and one about which a few hypotheses have emerged.

I also came to appreciate that this phenomenon trumps the marketing question of *"How can this be?"* although I've spent a fair amount of time deconstructing the elements of how passion brands come into being and maintain their status, and whether or not this is done consciously by consumers. Indeed, the "how" of passion brands is the backbone of this book.

But, the "thing behind the thing," the reason to look closely at passion brands, is the bottom line. We're talking about margin and profitability, the "no substitute will do" factor. A passion brand is not interchangeable with another that seems "roughly right." We willingly pay whatever the brand asks us to, and we go to extreme lengths to keep our personal inventory well stocked. In this way a passion brand fundamentally contradicts the "why pay more?" ethos of modern retailing.

It is important to make the distinction between being a passion brand devotee and being what marketers term an "early adopter" of a brand. By this they mean a consumer who sort of surfs the world looking for novelty, the new, finding the joy not only in the brand but also being the first to have it, or whatever comes next. Technology products often attract these folks.

But genuine passion brands can be new or old, big or small. They just must be alive, growing, and exciting, and they must serve as a potent form of self-communication. We are telling ourselves and people we know or meet about ourselves through the brands, not simply the acquisition of the latest incarnation of new, hot, or hard to get. The brand is a badge, of course. But the search I went on with this book was not about the need for novelty; it is about the loyal and passionate devotion to certain versions of key brands to tell the world about ourselves.

Early adopter brands resist growth; part of their joy is the insider status they confer. Indeed, early adopters typically try not to advocate for these brands, worrying that broad distribution will muddy the brand's exceptionality and, therefore, meaning. Thus, a new, tiny favorite restaurant is not talked about in an attempt to preserve its insider status for in-the-know customers; a boutique hotel never advertises that it's actually opened, preferring to cater to a select clientele; for instance, when Google launched its Gmail service, one had to be "recommended" by a friend in order to use it. And even though just about anyone can get a Gmail account now, it's a great example of exclusivity as dramatic entrance strategy. Such brands often become fads or at least remain small by design since their growth trajectory is suppressed by the gravitational tug of exceptionality.

HOW DO WE DECIDE WHICH BRANDS ARE PASSION BRANDS AND WHICH ARE FADS OR MERELY SUCCESSFULLY MARKETED?

As I began to research this idea—that we are forming relationships to brands that are more powerful than those we hold with many of the people in our lives—I set about measuring how much passion various brands actually generate. My thought was straightforward: Make a funnel into which we'd pour all the major brands that exist at the beginning of the twenty-first century in America. Create criteria that would not only weed out the failing but also the merely successful, and then tag the megabrands that may serve as linchpins of the retail shelves but don't make a claim on our hearts. I wanted to end up with a short list of passion brands and from there figure out what they have in common.

BRANDS THAT ROSE TO THE TOP IN THE INITIAL SCREEN

Porsche	Levis	Nike
Nissan	True Religion	Aerosoles
Cadillac	Rocawear	New Balance
Harley-Davidson		
Jeep		
	Tide	Turbo Tax
	Crest	Quicken
Marlboro	Clorox	
Newport	Pledge	Puffs
Camel		
	Neutrogena	General Electric
Sony	Johnson & Johnson	Whirlpool
Sharp	Suave	Kenmore
Bang & Olufsen	Dove	
Bose	Avon	Snickers
		Dove
AriZona Iced Tea	Target	Kraft
Jack Daniel's	Nordstrom	Hellmann's Mayonnaise
Starbucks	Wegmans	Hershey's Kisses
	Trader Joe's	NASCAR
Apple	Costco	New England Patriots
Motorola		Green Bay Packers

If the premise is correct and we are turning to brands for relationships that rival bonds forged with friends, family, and colleagues, then there are tremendous implications for business and society. The repercussions of this thesis could well echo beyond the one or two brands we love and love to talk about, and even suggest that we should be as passionate about having them in our investment portfolios as we are about having them in our pantries, pockets, and purses.

I made a few assumptions to launch this investigation into the emotional connection that is the driving element of such brands. First, to determine a short list I decided to seek brands to which consumers spontaneously acknowledge an emotional connection. To do this, I turned to a quantitative research firm (International Communications Research) that fielded questions to a broad base of consumers. Essentially, we asked an open-ended series of questions, using my definition of a passion brand, to determine if any sprang spontaneously to mind.

That process created a list of fifty or so brands. The next step was to index these brands to their share of market figures, or share of voice. Share of market is the ranking of sales a brand has within its category. Tide, for example, might have a 50 percent share of the detergent market. Its share of voice is the amount of advertising it uses to tell its story, as compared with all advertising in the detergent category. A brand like Marlboro, for example, also garners a roughly 50 percent share with its cigarettes and has used historically high levels of advertising. These types of megabrands would automatically come to the top of many lists. I was more interested in the brands that haven't been shouting their stories for decades and yet manage to earn a loyal and highly vocal, enthusiastic following.

My thinking here was we could make a case that we could find passion brands among those small brands, those that are less well known but mentioned as frequently as the big, well-advertised, enduring brands. This eliminated about twenty brands that are arguably well known and loved, but only because they'd been around a long time. What surfaced were about thirty that really out-performed in their category, independent of advertising spending or longevity.

BRANDS LOVED BY 1,000 FRIENDS AND COLLEAGUES

Prius	**Tide**	**Trader Joe's**
Jeep		**Wegmans**
Cadillac		**Wawa**
Volkswagen	*American Idol*	Fresh Direct
Porsche	*30 Rock*	
Prius		
Mini-Cooper		
	Absolut	
Krispy Kreme	**Jack Daniel's**	
Camel	Belvedere	
Sony	Elizabeth Arden's	
Bang & Olufsen	**Hellmann's Mayonnaise**	
Aerosoles	Amanresorts	
	Midwest Airlines	
Steve & Barry's		
Lord & Taylor	Sauvignon Blanc	
	Merlot	
Apple		
	Chemistry.com	

The next step was to double-check this list with an admittedly more subjective survey of roughly a thousand marketing professionals and friends, asking them for their candidates for passion brands. It was interesting to note that most of the brands my friends and colleagues nominated were on the original list, so the resulting thirty or so were doubly vetted. Late-night conversations and e-mail exchanges provided some colorful commentary on why certain brands rise to the level of passion.

Beyond the intense emotional connection between brand and user that is the marker of passion brands, there seemed to be two or three additional factors to which I'd need to pay attention. Passion is hardly passive, so I assumed I could whittle down my list further if I understood which of those brands have a living, breathing, interactive relationship with their consumers. A genuine passion brand seems alive, dynamic, and evolves with the needs and desires of its users. The way one cool rapper ties his Nikes, for example, impacts how Nikes will be tied—or left untied—in the future by others who have seen him and want to mimic him. The way one group of teenage boys wears their Levi's low on the waist tells others how to wear theirs, regardless of what mothers or teachers have to say about it.

There really is a vital, viral life force to these brands. We can have a relationship with them because they seem to be alive, whether it's how they seem to get smarter as we use them (Google) or how using them can create a sense of instant community with others (Starbucks). In a wide variety of ways passion brands seem to respond to us in real time and be in a jet-propelled evolutionary process. They simply do not stand still.

I went looking for this vitality with two terrific graduate business students at Wake Forest University in order to create an index of "Brand Consumer Involvement." Vanessa Capobianco and Claire McLeod assessed the life force of passion brand candidates via dialogue between brand and consumer (and back again) as tracked by mentions in third-party zones such as Facebook and MySpace, as well as the number of Google and other search engine hits. Editorial coverage and movie placements were also taken into account here in order to acknowledge the ways in which brands seemingly begin to spontaneously combust onto our landscape, although it is a combustion often paid for by brand marketers that arrives courtesy of public relations firms and movie companies. Sometimes though, the passion brand becomes a "real" story, generating discovery and coverage just because it's interesting.

From this process, we culled twenty or so passion brand finalists, some of which had been on the original list of fifty and some of which supplanted those.

Another marker of emotional commitment is the personal need or desire to make a recommendation—a *forceful* recommendation, as in "You've *got* to try this!"

BRANDS THAT ROSE TO THE TOP FOR LIFE FORCE ENGAGEMENT	
Apple	Disney
Sony	American Express
Starbucks	**NASCAR**
Folger's	
Target	**Camel**
Nordstrom	
Craig's List	**Absolut**
Whole Foods	
Toys"R"Us	**Kraft**
Cadillac	
BMW	
Acura	
Infiniti	
Jeep	
AriZona Iced Tea	

How much did a brand's vitality rely on powerful, personal endorsement? Of course there could be advertising to generate awareness, but what revved the engine of a passion brand would surely be the engaged enthusiasm, the evangelism, and the proselytizing of its devoted fans.

To understand this dimension, I worked with my colleague Hal Goldberg, who hypnotizes consumers to explore the hidden recesses of their attitudes and opinions. Hypnotism may seem like a, well, weird way to gain legitimate consumer understanding, particularly consumer understanding that can be applied to broad cross-sections of the population. It is a technique that we have used with remarkable success, however. We use it to search for the archetype, the deep meaning, of both the category and the brand we're exploring.

Hypnosis allows us to get beyond the traditional barriers in conducting consumer focus groups. Such two-hour sessions bring together specific types of people (working women, stay-at-home moms, do-it-yourself dads, thrill-of-the-grill enthusiasts, for example) to discuss attitudes and opinions about current or new products or advertising approaches. A moderator leads the group through a discussion while her or his colleagues sit behind a one-way mirror and watch the process unfold.

Once you've sat through enough of such groups, you know the hobbles. There is always one person who wants to lead, even dominate the discussion. There is usually a shy one or two who won't say a word. There is frequently a sense of trying to please the moderator, or of figuring out the "right" or "wrong" response. There is often a "piling on" process that moves the individual thoughts into an oftentimes artificial consensus.

A traditional focus group may work for some situations, but my strong preference over the years has become hypnosis. When he works with me, Hal probes the same six questions. What are their first, most powerful and most recent experiences in the category? What are their first, most powerful and most recent experiences with the brand? Since everyone's memories are uniquely his or her own, there is no dominant player or shy ones, no "right" or "wrong" answers, no "piling on." Each one shares, in turn, and from these individual responses we can glean the meaning behind the meaning, the deep power and promise that categories and brands bring to consumers. Once we have that, we can determine how better to deliver it, and that's where genuine brand breakthroughs can emerge.

For the passion brand search, we recruited men and women whose passion brands were among those twenty that survived on the list to explore what it means to recommend something to a friend, colleague, or family member. We were searching for the ways that passion brand recommendations emerge and evolve, or not, as they radiate outward from one enthusiast. Where there social or perhaps personal risks involved in making powerful recommendations? What was the social or psychic reward that made making such recommendations important enough to overcome those risks?

We also wanted to separate "beloved brands" from "I can't live without it and neither should you" brands. I may love Quaker Oats oatmeal because I grew up with it and it always takes me back to cold winter mornings before school and the warmth that stayed with me and conveyed love, family, and care, as well as nutrition. But I am unlikely to want to convert you to love it, too. I'm willing to let that brand remain personal and private. A genuine passion brand refuses to remain warm and toasty, not to mention private, in my memory. There's something about a passion brand that demands consumer conversion, and my mission was to find that something.

One of the crucial findings during the hypnosis sessions was the identification of the passion brand archetype. By this I mean, what does the idea of recommending a brand stand for in the mind of the consumer? What is its larger significance? There must be something more than just taste, flavor, convenience, or other performance attributes rather than merely its functional description that generates emotional testimonials.

For example, when I recommend Fresh Direct, I certainly speak about its functional benefits, such as the freshness and variety of the produce, meats, and dairy products, as well as the ability to order it anytime, the online convenience, and the courtesy of the delivery people. But I go well beyond that, describing the great dinners with family and friends it helps provide, the company's ability to find my daughter's favorite cereal, even the immediacy of its refund process if there's anything wrong with the order. The Fresh Direct brand has delivered an emotional benefit to me. My enthusiasm is tethered to that *feeling*. I want to share it with friends so that they can enjoy that *feeling* as well.

Once we identified the larger emotional terrain in which such brands move, I wanted to figure out what consumers "get" from giving a recommendation. What's in it for them?

We went looking for the value of brand recommendation, namely, its deep significance, and the proof, as in how we know we've gotten the experience we're looking for when we recommend a brand.

Remember the original (non-Webster) definition of passion brand I'd stumbled upon: a brand you recommend to friends wholeheartedly, even evangelically—so much so that if they don't embrace it as vigorously as you do, you perceive a cloud over *their* heads, blocking the sunshine of the brand. As we proceeded, I began to understand the entire issue of the cloud over their heads. Why does a treasured brand recommendation carry such a significant emotional valence? As I sat listening to person after person under hypnosis describe personal delight in certain brands—and the serious irritation when a recommendation was not adopted or appreciated—it became clear.

When we recommend a brand to someone, it is like a gift. We are giving a friend, a colleague, a family member the gift of a prized possession—our recommendation. How do we know they've received it as we meant it? They say thank you, just as they would with a gift. They then tell a small anecdote that illustrates their excitement and enthusiasm, just as they would with a gift they'd truly enjoyed. We all know the delight when a gift is appreciated and used, becoming a significant element in the receiver's life and the object through which we forge and deepen the relationship. Unhappily, we probably also know the disappointment, perhaps irritation, that arises when we find out that the gift has been "re-gifted," or at least not really enjoyed. To refuse to accept or adopt a brand recommendation evokes an equivalent feeling of annoyance. It's the rejection of an admittedly different type of gift, one that is supposed to be prized because of its profoundly personal nature.

I'm highlighting some of the key findings here, but I came to believe that this voice of the consumer is so central to understanding the passion brand phenomenon that I've inserted their perspectives between each chapter to help bring to life their emotional connections to key brands. These are verbatim quotes to help readers gain their own understanding of the power such brands, brand memories, and their meanings exerted in our emotional lives as well as in our transactional, buying, consuming, and buying again lives. I've included in these sections, titled *What We Talk about When We Talk about Brands*, comments from the people who use and love key brands. These descriptions of the brands come from their advocates while under hypnosis. I hope it helps readers begin to fathom the truly amazing depth of emotional content that is emblematic of our relationships with passion brands. I hope, too, that it begins to suggest the reasons to work hard and systematically to develop and grow passionate brand enthusiasts, which, of course, is the purpose of this book.

Men and women in the groups approached brand evangelism differently. Women tended to recommend a wide variety of new things from trusted brands, ranging from Tide-to-Go to new Folgers Aroma Seal Chocolate Silk, confections to the Apple iPhone, the shopping experience at Lord & Taylor and television shows such as *Desperate Housewives*. In short, women were agnostic about what categories they were passionate about and whether or not the brand was new or had been around forever.

As Faith Popcorn pointed out her in book *EVEolution*, "Women want a relationship and men want a transaction." This credo certainly proved to be true in the passion brand context. What seemed to annoy men the most was when the recipient of their recommendation wanted to continue the dialogue, rather than just take it, say thank you, and adopt it as their own. "I told him what GPS system to get and where to go to get it installed, but he wanted to keep talking about it," one guy recalled with irritation. "He just wouldn't stop asking questions."

Again and again, guys would talk about the friend they recommended a GPS system to and then got irritated with the friend when he needed help to install or use it. They didn't want to engage that deeply in the recommendation: they just wanted the acknowledgment of their leadership and for the friend to "figure it out," as they had.

Take another example of a fellow who'd recommended a GPS navigation system to a buddy: "He bought the wrong model and he hated it. He didn't listen to me and then he had the audacity to say, 'You got me into this, you have to get me out!' It was so annoying. He just kept at it. I finally said, 'Don't you have anything else to do but bother me about this?'"

Guys were different, too, in the narrow list of things they'd bother recommending: high-tech gizmos, car stuff, flat-panel TVs, GPS systems, and more flat-panel TVs. And woe to those who weren't appreciative. One fellow was particularly memorable about his flat-panel TV.

"I had just gotten it," he recalled under hypnosis. "I'd seen what my boss had gotten and I wanted the same thing. He'd done a lot of research and I knew I could trust his decision. So I went out and got it. Put it up in the den and was ready for the play-offs. I invited my best friend over. I had ordered pizza. I had chips and beer, and I was ready. I turned the set on and I wanted him to like it as much as I did and to want one the way I had. But he said, 'The picture's not so great, really.' I was upset. In a little while I told him I didn't feel like watching anymore, I wasn't in the mood anymore. I told him he'd better leave. I was going to take a nap. He left. He knew something was wrong. He knew I was upset. I didn't have to say anything. He knew. The next day he apologized, but it was still kind of ruined. We're not as good friends really. I knew he was jealous, but that didn't make it okay."

Interestingly, men seemed to recommend more exclusively to men, and women to women just the same. Although one newlywed fellow recalled his disappointment when his wife laughed at his enthusiasm for one new food. "I told my wife about Breakstone Fat Free Sour Cream. She just hated it. She said it was disgusting. I was shocked. It changes the way we eat together. I don't feel free to make recommendations anymore."

So feelings get hurt, or expertise is extolled. Something happens in that triangulation among the giver of the recommendation, the recommended product or service, and the receiver. And it sure is fascinating to watch once you've broken the code of what it all means.

What these groups also showed me was that for some passion brands there seemed to be a "deal breaker" role, as in "I wouldn't marry someone who used Miracle Whip on his sandwich." One woman described a blind date she'd gone on. It was just for drinks, after having met each other online, chatting back and forth for several weeks, and talking on the phone for hours on several occasions.

"I met him at a bar and the waitress came over," she recalled. "I ordered a Belvedere on the rocks with wedges of lime. He asked for 'a beer,' and when the waitress asked him what kind, he said, 'Oh, whatever is on tap.' I knew immediately it would never work. He just didn't have an appreciation of detail." In this case, the lack of a passion brand *sensibility* was at issue. It didn't have to be Belvedere, but she wanted him to have some sort of personal passion for what he was drinking.

Not all recommendations are created equal or last that long. Having a personal recommendation is a necessary but not sufficient marker of genuine passion. Hellmann's Mayonnaise is a litmus test for some folks, but others opt in and out of their brand relationships a bit more promiscuously, shall we say. Those for whom Hellmann's is the sine qua non of mayonnaise are passionate about Hellmann's; the others are simply engaged for a time with the brand.

I also knew I needed to confront head-on the resistance that nearly always came up when I discussed the passion brand definition with friends or colleagues. So often people told me, "There's no brand I feel *that* passionate about." It always seemed to me to be a defensive position, in opposition to the notion of a thing-obsessed consumer society. In discussion, I could pretty much always get them to admit, "Well, there is one brand I feel strongly about," but I needed to understand that initial wall of resistance.

When it was a friend I knew well, such as trend spotter Faith Popcorn, I could remind her of her enthusiasm for Louis

Licari and his hair salon and products. When she'd recommend to friends that they should "go see Louis," it was a gift from her to them—and when they didn't take the recommendation to heart, or worse, went and didn't come back raving, it did put a question mark over the friendship. I'd seen it happen. When I stated the case in that intensely personal context, she agreed. So could others to whom I made the case, based on my knowledge of their brand enthusiasms ranging from *Sex in the City* to Bumble Bee Tuna to Madonna. But initial reluctance to admit to passionate brand attachments that could trump personal ones intrigued me.

There is a universality to the experience of having the right stuff. What PC owner hasn't felt "dissed" on an airplane when firing up his laptop next to the cool guy with the iBook G4?

Rob Walker, who wrote *Buying In: The Secret Dialogue between What We Buy and Who We Are*, acknowledges this denial personally: When Nike bought Converse, Walker, a certified Chuck Taylor All Stars wearer since his teens, was devastated. His cooler-than-cool brand had been swooshed by Nike, "a symbol for suckers who take its 'Just Do It' bullying at face value. We can talk all we want about being brand-proof," says Walker, "but our behavior tells a different story."[1]

It was while watching the hypnosis groups that I began to realize that the resistance to the notion of questioning a personal relationship because of a bad brand review was at least as much of a shield, a defense against a painful memory or the embarrassment of a gift given and not appreciated, as it was the claimed triumph of friendship over consumerism.

One woman had her feelings hurt in the bathroom of an airport: "I was traveling with colleagues from work. I took out my lip gloss and I'd just been saying how wonderful it was and telling my co-workers to buy it because it was so long lasting and yet not very expensive. A co-worker came out from the stall, looked at the lip gloss and said, 'I hate that stuff,' and then she went on to bash it hard. It annoyed me and I thought it made me look bad in front of my peers."

From a young woman at work: "I love AriZona Diet Green Tea. My father likes it, too. I took it to work and my friends asked about it. I got some for them to try. I was sure they would like it the way my father had. But they didn't like it. It really annoyed me. I was so disappointed that they just didn't get it."

Or this from young woman who recommended coffee yogurt to her father: "He refused to even try it! I'm his daughter. He could have at least tried it, couldn't he? I mean, it's just yogurt. He likes coffee. He just wouldn't try it. I was so disappointed."

The emotional words come through nearly every anecdote: Disappointed. Annoyed. Upset. Shocked. Frustrated.

The goal is nearly always "to share the joy I felt" or "to let them in on how wonderful it is."

By this time, it began to feel as though passion brands were something like passionate relationships. There are those products with which we start out with a passion, but the ardor cools along the way and settles into something more like commitment and loyalty. Commitment and loyalty are good things, of course, but I wanted the reason why some brands are *just gotta have, drive all night, tell your friends* brands. They start out that way and they stay that way, as if thirty years into a relationship you still are swooning over the one you love.

Writing in the *Journal of Product and Brand Management*, Pamela Alreck and Robert B. Settle put it this way: "Whether it is between parent and child, friends, lovers, or consumer and brand, bonding is a process; not so much of war among rivals, but of courtship between suitor and beloved. Unlike a single

seduction or conquest, the courtship process includes identifi-
able phases—introduction, familiarity, then preference, and
finally, if successful, a loyalty that excludes relationships with
rival suitors."[2]

There is in the expression of brand passion something of
the thrill of a quest: I've gone out there into the marketplace
and was as confused and overwhelmed as you; I found a way
through it and I know the best answer. Follow me! Thus, the
confusion of the marketplace contributes to the quest and the
thrill. Indeed, there is a syntax to follow and it looks like this.

Think of the *confusion* we all confront when trying to
adopt a new technology or discern between brands of cell
phones or carriers, shoes or diamond rings, flat-panel TVs or
shampoos. The market is a perplexing place. We quickly

PASSION BRAND RITUAL

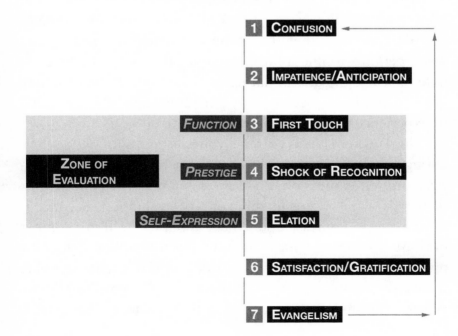

become *impatient* to make a decision in order to reduce the anxiety that uncertainty and the overwhelming amount of choices produce. So there's a sense of urgency, a deep desire to get to a resolution, and an *anticipation* of what the future holds once we've acquired the object of our desire. For some, the anxiety is an enjoyable part of the process and they can seemingly hold vast quantities of information in their minds as they evaluate options. For others, this process produces an untenable agony. But for all of us, there's a push to decide or move on.

If we opt to purchase, there's the *first touch* of the goods once we've acquired them. We are moving into a process I've come to think of as the *zone of evaluation*, through which a product moves from stranger to friend to passion brand. It must meet our expectations, of course, but then it must exceed them; it must surprise and delight us in order to engage us in a way that virtually forces us to share and spread the news.

We're home and are now in a more reflexive state of mind. We try on. We luxuriate in the feel. Occasionally, we rethink the purchase now that the shopping anxiety has passed and we're perhaps feeling a bit of remorse. In any event, we evaluate once again, congratulating or chastising, as the case may be. The first touch becomes the portal through which we pass to experience the object as owned, as mine.

This is where it gets extremely interesting, since we're evaluating on three aspects of the brand experience: function, prestige, and self-expression. First, the thing must work and work thrillingly while we're in this zone of evaluation. Second, it must make an impressive statement about itself. In this context prestige doesn't just mean it's an expensive choice; it must make a statement of cultural values, which could be smart (Suave shampoo), environmentally aware (Toyota Prius), convenient (Fresh Direct)—any of a host of image attributes.

Third, it needs to help me say something about myself. I'm going to badge myself with this brand, after all, using it as social currency expended in discussion, recommendation, and even personal proselytizing.

In the best situations, we experience a *shock of recognition*: this is mine. We wonder, how did I live without it? It fits in the hand, or it tastes fabulous, or it's the perfect pair of shoes to go with the outfit, *at last!* Whatever it is, this sense of acquisition, of the thing becoming mine, is where real passion starts to ignite.

We move from that first pleasure into a *state of elation*. We made the right decision! We are thrilled with it and eager to try it out in many contexts of our lives. Wearing it and sharing it, surely. And also, caring for it. It's ours.

We move out of the *zone of evaluation* and into an information acquisition mode. Now we need the words to explain our newfound passion. We're in *satisfaction and gratification*. The adage that the only people who actually read car ads are the people who just bought the car is true for many categories. We need the backstory. Who made it? How was it made? Under what conditions? Just as when it comes time to introduce a new lover to our family, we need details to share.

Finally, we're ready for brand *evangelism*. We're not going to just introduce our passion brand to our mothers and fathers; we're going to spread the word, the good news of what we've found to anyone who will listen. We're going to bring the news back and help alleviate all those who are in the confusing state we so recently escaped.

Surely the forging of a passion brand has to do with a feeling of gratitude, that the brand has somehow understood you, anticipated your needs, and responded to them in a way that makes you want to sing its praises, to give the gift of that brand to others and have them share in your enthusiasm, to join your brand community. For the truly brand-smitten, imitation is the sincerest form of consumer flattery.

More important, the postevangelism period is one of brand buzz that will ultimately lead us back to a market that, because it's constantly reinventing itself, will emerge in time as confusing to us once more. Think, for example, of buying an iPod. At first it's exciting and gratifying, and with hindsight, pretty simple. It was a new idea, and it came in one version and some colors. We make our choice, learn the process for downloading songs, then begin to evangelize, attempting to convert others to this new and thrilling product. But then, a couple of years into the development of iPodNation, our battery runs out and it's just time to go back to the store. But which store? An Apple store or any of a dozen or more chains that now carry other versions of MP3 players? And which player? One just like our old one, or the Nano, or the Shuffle? Which color? Which case? Whoosh! We're confused and need to chart a new way through the maze. Once we've done it, of course, we've earned additional credentials to help friends and family rely on our recommendation. Indeed, in many cases, they would not dare enter a store without it—or us.

The brand doesn't stop there but continues to "be the same and yet different every day," the way a Starbucks at its best surprises and delights us with new music, T-mobile hot spots, and emerging writers while maintaining its focus on coffee in all its aroma-driven glory and million variations. It's a matter of ownership. Apple, too, needs to ensure that while other MP3 players like the Microsoft Zune may come and go, iPod remains the gold standard, the purchase decision you don't need to explain to anybody once you've made it.

When we return to the confusion of the marketplace, nothing else comes close to our passion brand, no Circe's song seduces us to the competition since so firmly tethered are we to the mast of our brand. A genuine passion brand must not have an acceptable alternative: No substitute will do. "If I can't have Hellmann's Mayonnaise on my BLT, I'll skip lunch or have a salad."

So off to the market we go. But now we're seasoned, highly involved consumers. We know more, we ask different questions, our identity has begun to be forged as lay experts because we have evangelized. We're now among the people to whom others turn for expert opinion—on shoes, films, restaurants, mountain bikes, or airline travel—whatever territory we've staked out.

WHY IS THIS HAPPENING NOW?

When I left my position as president of Faith Popcorn's Brain-Reserve, I resolved to work on issues of pressing business strategy for a limited roster of companies that found themselves at a crossroads. I no longer wanted to be in the business of monitoring consumer trends and using them to predict consumer behavior for the next ten years. But when confronted with a multilateral phenomenon such as passion brands, I really had to try to assess some root causes. Thus, part 2 reports on the cultural forces that are currently propelling passion brands.

I believe the topic of brand passion is particularly important to consider in difficult economic times. When pressures mount on companies' bottom lines, they typically look first to the expense side of products, both in the development and the marketing of them. The opportunity that a brand passion presents is the opportunity to conscript willing and enthusiastic consumers to spend their financial and social currency on those brands, exhorting friends and family to follow suit.

So what are the passion brands we uncovered? One wants a drum roll. However, without any more drama, here they are.

Three types of beverages rose to the top: Jack Daniel's in the world of spirits, American wines, and Starbucks. I know that American wines may seem more like a category, as in French bread, rather than a brand. But in the rarefied world of wines, becoming a serious entrant meant first legitimizing the region the way California rose to the challenge worthy of close scrutiny. There is little conventional brand passion in wine since the constraints of the varying vintages and wine producers limit availability of one offering to rise up year after year. So wine enthusiasts (we're not speaking here of Blue Nun aficionados, after all) have relied on the names of importers, the style or region (e.g., Bordeaux or Champagne), vintages, price, or in some cases names like Maison Louis Jadot or Rothschild to help drinkers make and discuss their choices. American wines came late to the party and how they did it— commanding upward of $150 for some bottles at the winery— is worthy of study.

As for food? Krispy Kreme (yes, still, despite the hot- and cold-running enthusiasm of Wall Street, conglomerates, and franchisees). And Kraft. Every generation forms a passionate attachment to one of its brands: Mac & Cheese, Oreos, or Mallomars, which rose to the top, again and again. But interestingly from this perspective, it was the name Kraft that came up, not the product or brand name but the actual corporate parent's name had somehow gotten the halo from these beloved foods. And Hellmann's Mayonnaise. For scores of people, nothing else came close.

- Automotive: The Mini Cooper, Toyota Prius, Jeep, and Cadillac (what a turnaround for this once decrepit brand)

- Cigarettes: Camel
- Electronics: Sony
- Shoes: Converse
- Clothes: Lord & Taylor
- Computing: Apple (no surprise there, I suspect)
- Cleaning: Tide, with a special emphasis on Tide-to-Go
- Grocery: Wegmans, Wawa, Fresh Direct
- Online dating: Chemistry.com (from Match.com)
- Sports teams: San Francisco 49ers and New England Patriots
- Entertainment: *30 Rock*
- Airline: Midwest Airlines
- Retailing: Amazon

Then began the process of searching out the information, both from the quantitative analysis of publicly available information and through the far-more-granular approach of going into the grocery stores, malls, main streets, and Web sites to explore the passion brands of twenty-first-century America. I found other brands along the way that piqued my interest: Red Bull, Absolut Vodka, IKEA, Amanresorts, Peet's, GEICO, Volkswagen, Virgin, Google, Mt. Olive Pickles, Disney, and Pixar. I'll share insights from some of these explorations as well.

I also wanted to get closer to understand these brands from the inside. I interviewed corporate, strategic, and marketing executives who were intimately involved with the development of the passion brands on which I decided to focus. These were wide-ranging interviews designed to get at how they saw the brands' successes and failures, how they explain it to themselves and others. What makes a passion brand tick to the beat of popular culture not just for a moment, not as a simple fad but as a genuine, heartfelt, in some cases lifelong and generational love affair?

My final checkpoint in writing about passion brands was to do what I came to think of as a simple "gut check." Passion is personal. I think it is fair to factor in personal reactions and anecdotes to various passion brands, in some cases where the passion evoked was one of rage. While I don't dwell on this in detail here, it's fair to note that Starbucks, any brand of cigarette, virtually every sports team, and political candidates are capable of eliciting passion on both sides of the love/hate divide. Oil companies have a passionate following of, well, furious critics.

I believe I found what I was looking for: what I call the seven accelerators of passion brands, when the passion is love. I hit upon a number of fascinating stories, all of which I share with you here to illustrate these seven points. I also unearthed some intriguing theories about why brands are playing this remarkably relational role in our lives.

Having defined and documented a passion brand, and with a sense of the cultural forces shaping our love affairs, I will focus next on the accelerators that help forge the consumer's passion for a brand. The following chapters go into the common denominators I found.

The model I use at the beginning of each of these chapters illustrates the fundamental importance of the seven accelerators of passion brands I've identified and when in the process each plays its vital role in the formation of consumer passion. This is worth dwelling upon: There is a syntax, a consumer experience syntax that must be honored. As you'll see, the steplike progression through which a passion brand is forged in the consumer's mind is not at all the same as it is developed in the maker's, creator's, or manufacturer's mind. What I detail here is the way each element must be sequenced—revealed even—to develop an evolving and deepening consumer relationship.

- **Work the Worldview, Not Age, Race, or Gender**
  The passion brands I studied rarely seem to target consumers in a traditional way, as in women eighteen to thirty-four. More often, they identify shared values about the world and how it works and then illustrate how the brand also shares in that vision.

- **Differentiate on Design**
  Consumers respond to clever, intuitive products. Great design engages. There's a joy in a well-designed idea that can trump other performance features. We just want to get our hands on it.

- **Hire Passionistas as Brand Stewards**
  Nothing brings a brand down more quickly than an interchangeable parts philosophy in the recruitment, hiring, and rewarding of the people behind it. Careerists who jump from one company or industry to another on their way to ever more senior posts may be building their own brand, but they will neither feel nor fuel the passion. Passion isn't static in brands or in people. Once people have become passionate about your brand, it takes true passionistas to ensure that the brand continues to grow and evolve in exciting, relevant ways. Don't take your consumers or their passion for your brand for granted.

- **Know They Know You Need Them**
  We are in a tremendously aware marketing epoch. Our vocabulary and our humor are shaped by an "insider's" sensibility to marketing and the codependence of the brand/consumer liaison.
  As I tell my clients, "There are no unfocused group

people left in the country." It is part of the reason I use hypnosis to get beyond the sheer "been there, done that" savvy of modern consumers. So get out and watch people in bars, malls, grocery stores, movies, sports events, regardless of the category you are in. Talk to them. Follow them while they shop. Engage them. Notice that you are one of them.

- **Democratize the Brand**
  Brand monoliths don't live and grow. Real engagement comes from mutating because you are responding to the beat of the people who love you. Let them in. Easier said than done if you're a physical product sold in a physical store and not a Web-based entity, but still.

  The ability of the consumer to have it "my way" is a tremendous engine of ownership. Starbucks, with its "mocha cappuccino double-shot skinny" ethos, is the poster child of this tactic for five-dollar caffeine in a cup, and so is the Scion with its personalization of everything from engine horsepower and pin striping to stick shift knobs, all for seventeen thousand dollars.

- **Mine the Mythos**
  Passion brands have a heritage and they respect it. They know what is in the DNA of the brand and how far they can and should go without putting their genetic code at risk. This doesn't mean they are old and stodgy, just that they know how their personality can legitimately evolve.

- **Brand the Buzz**
  In saying this I don't mean that companies should hire a bunch of twenty-somethings to dress in black and ask for your product by name in clubs. This is about being

genuinely interesting and engaging, being a brand that people want to talk about, gossip about, and share with friends. What would *Sex and the City* do?

Chapter 9 of part 1 is my prescription: I'm applying these seven laws of passion branding to a couple of products in order to help make the case to you, and to help you advocate for making your business model a passionate one.

Just one more note. As you read this book, look at what type of product categories have forged passion brands and which ones haven't. There are many beverage companies, numerous manufacturers of computers, consumer electronics, and automobiles, and lots of sports teams. There are many food products, but no fast-food entrants on our list. Some site-specific resorts or incredibly upscale leisure destinations, but there are no hotel chains, and only one small airline, Midwest Air (no, not even JetBlue or Southwest Airlines were mentioned even once).

I looked at oil companies, for example, but there is clearly not one of them about which we care at all. That's fertile "white space" to my mind. British Petroleum may have tried, but no brand rises above our disdain for the industry. (It's amazing to consider that the comparably vilified tobacco industry still spawns a brand, Camel, treasured by many.)

Single-vision companies, such as Starbucks and Google, seem far better equipped to manage cultivation of passion. Of course, everyone stumbles now and again, and we shall see if Starbucks can recover its footing. One of the most interesting benefits of growing a passion brand, which may help Starbucks out, is that the consumer is remarkably forgiving. Daryl Brewster, former head of Nabisco and Krispy Kreme, described this to me in detail in our interview. "We'd get letters from consumers about problems with Oreo packaging or some such," he recalled. "They'd say, 'It's probably something I did, maybe I opened it incorrectly, but I wanted you to know.' That kind of thing. An expression of genuine care for the brand. Almost protective."

We'll delve into this more later, but it's an important and under-the-radar benefit, this notion that consumers feel a genuine sense of caring for passion brands and want to shield them from harm.

Now then, onward into our findings. The first accelerator of passion brands: appeal to a worldview, not a demographic.

Chapter 2
WORK THE WORLDVIEW, NOT THE AGE, RACE, OR GENDER

W hy do fools fall in love? Let's ask the experts: Chemistry.com is the online dating service launched by Match.com to help ignite and deliver the intangible "chemical attraction" we all hope for in a relationship. Starting in 2004, working with the then-new CEO Jim Safka, advertising guru Adam Hanft reasoned that something was missing in most online offerings and that state-of-the-art research into human emotions was required. Together they sought out Helen Fisher, professor at Princeton University and best-selling author of books such as *Why We Love*.

According to Mandy Ginsberg, vice president and general manager of Chemistry.com, "Meeting Helen has changed my life, as well as my profession. She just knows so much about why we love who we love that it's been fascinating personally, as well as in the service of creating and building this brand. It's no coincidence that we've become the fastest growing site: People are thrilled to be associated with products and companies that share their values."[1]

BRANDING PROCESS STEP 1

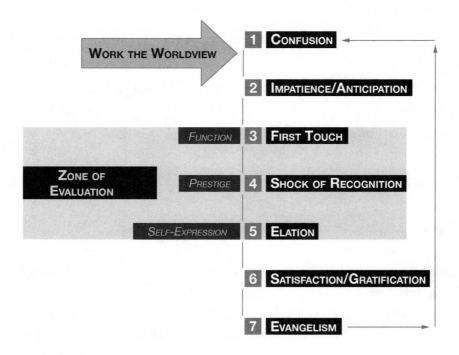

This sharing of values began with values not shared: Chemistry.com was created to respond to the perceived flaws in the fundamental concept of a competitor, eHarmony.com. As best I can determine the chronology, it was 2000 or thereabouts when eHarmony entered the market and was siphoning members away from Match.com, which had grown and thrived as a "dating site." Those at eHarmony characterized it as a "marriage site." Founded by Neil Clark Warren, it had been influenced by the Christian teachings of Rev. James Dobson, and three of Warren's books were published by Dobson's Focus on the Family. Warren boasts a divinity degree as well as psychologist credentials.

Thus, it did not support "illegal unions," in other words, gay marriage and sex outside of marriage. People seeking those relationships are rejected by the site. The "Weed-Outs" roughly correlate to 16 percent of participants, including others who flunk his twenty-nine-point personality quiz embedded in a two-hundred-plus question "test." Warren's take on reasons for rejection from the site is "experience based," as he explains that the bulk of his thirty-five years of research has been with heterosexual couples. That, plus the legal issue. "We really don't want to participate in something illegal," he told *USA Today* in 2005.

"We did the math," explains Ginsberg, "and realized that once you filled out the eHarmony four-hundred-question survey, about one million people got rejected—just imagine people getting up the nerve to go online and then, sorry! Nobody here for you. That's harsh. We thought this was really, really wrong. So, we started talking with Helen because of her theory of the complementary. She created a test that gets at what type of person you are and what type of person would be a good complementary match: someone with whom you'd have immediate and long-lasting chemistry. Certain personality types gravitate to other personality types."

Helen's process includes scores of questions, some posed in the form of a classic SAT multiple-choice quiz and some with brief essays or drawings built in. Are you an explorer, negotiator, builder, perhaps a director? You don't have to know the answer, the algorithm of the site will analyze your answers and serve up matches for you to pursue. One element they push: get to that first meeting as quickly as possible and then come back and report, thus the site will get smarter and smarter about finding Mr. or Ms. Right.

Fisher is quick to admit, as she points out in the Chemistry.com interview Q&A, awareness of these four personality groups can be said to go back nearly three millennia. "Many of the questions on the site are designed to establish the degree to which you are these various types," writes Fisher. "Of course, we are all a vast mix of *all* of these chemical components (and many others). And we are all unique individuals. But people do seem to fall into broad general categories—types that even Plato and Aristotle recorded some 2,500 years ago. And scientists now think that some 50 percent of one's personality has a genetic and hormonal basis.

"I also have questions designed to establish which chemical types you tend to be attracted to. Last, we ask you what you are looking for in a mate. And using your various answers, the folks at Chemistry.com and I hope to introduce you to individuals who will not only spark your brain circuitry for romantic love but also keep that passion percolating for years."

Helen Fisher's mission at Chemistry.com is to make that lasting passion easier for us to find. She has studied more than twenty-eight thousand matches generated by the site and describes her perspective as "watching Nature's basic laws of attraction unfold." In this worldview, it's all about neurochemical drivers: dopamine, testosterone, estrogen, and serotonin. There are certain crucial questions that helped her through the phases of scientific legitimacy: Is it valid? Is it reliable? Is it viable? At each stage of her inquiry she became more and more astute as to the precise phrasing of each question until, as she puts it, "I'll never change a word of this questionnaire."[2]

The high-dopamine individual is the explorer type, and goes for someone equally high on dopamine. Ditto for high-serotonin people: they are the builders and they like to be around other builders. High-estrogen people, on the other hand, are attracted to their opposites, the high-testosterone individuals, and vice versa.

"There are good evolutionary rationales for this," she tells me over the phone as we renew an acquaintance that goes back a least a decade. "It's logical. Explorers have high levels of dopamine and are comfortable with each other; builders, with high serotonin, are attracted to other builders. Both types need encouragement, understanding, and expertise; they get that best from people more like themselves. With high estrogen, you're a negotiator, often conciliatory, articulate, and socially adroit. You'll be attracted to [people] with high testosterone because they are directors, commanding, in charge, and forceful. And they'll need you because of your social skills, which will help them, since they can be didactic and curt."

To forestall the inevitable discussion of "my computerized relationship algorithm is better than your computerized relationship algorithm," Chemistry.com makes its values a centerpiece of the proposition.

"We have a brand that is nonjudgmental," says Ginsberg. "We're not going to tell you who to love or how to love. We're the opposite of eHarmony.com. People want to be associated with products and companies that share their values. Somewhere else I might have gotten fired for our first campaign, but the numbers went through the roof. We attract a left of center, progressive, urban person. We went out with those values and what we stood for. We believed the people would come. Sure enough we attracted those people: 30 percent with PhDs and masters degrees. We have 4.5 million people who have registered with us. We've obviously tapped into a worldview."

The brand's embrace of technology, talent, and tolerance has earned it other accolades as well, including an Effie and a GLAAD Award. Effie Awards are given by the advertising industry for "Ideas that Work." GLAAD is the Gay and Lesbian Alliance Against Defamation. Each year GLAAD honors those members of the media and advertising community who it believes are worthy of recognition and honor for "fair, accurate, and inclusive representation of the lesbian, gay, bisexual and transgender community and the issues that affect their lives."

Chemistry.com's first campaign was all about a reaction to eHarmony.com's basic proposition—and those one million people who had been "rejected." Chemistry.com's TV ads showed really cute actors, speaking to the camera and describing themselves as pretty good people but who had been rejected by eHarmony.com. The tagline: "Come to Chemistry.com. And, come as you are."

It struck a nerve. But as Ginsberg points out as I speak with her, it was a launch campaign. "We used eHarmony as the foil to establish ourselves. Like launching a soft drink against Coke. Who are we and what do we stand for? We're not about a lovely couple on the white screen. In our print ads, we'd show a beach with a sign saying, 'No gays on beach, May through September,' or a hotel with a sign reading, 'No premarital sex.' Then we'd ask, 'Don't want to live under eHarmony's rules?'"

By the beginning of 2008, Chemistry.com started to stand on its own instead of playing off the reference to eHarmony. With several years of experience (and thousands of successful matches), it could show real couples who were able to make a real-world commitment: "I promise to love you, even though your family's crazy."

"We went to real couples," recalls Ginsberg, explaining one of their ad spots to me. "Some are straight; one is a male gay couple walking through the grocery store, and one of the guys puts his hand on the other guy's hand. Sure, we heard from some people who were appalled by that on national television, but hey! We're marketing to people who share our values and ours are the values of inclusion and acceptance. You don't change what you stand for because somebody objects. You just keep doing what you're doing and hope that the vast numbers of people will be attracted to your proposition. We're on schedule to have our five millionth person register in the summer of 2008, and that's pretty fantastic."

Chemistry.com is clearly marketing to a mind-set and doing it at a pretty aggressive rate, considering that the site was launched in February 2006. To be clear, of course, eHarmony is also marketing to a worldview: just a radically different one compared to Chemistry.com.

"We are in era of full transparency," writes Adam Hanft on his blog on the Huffington Post. It's Adam's agency (Hanft Raboy Partners) that created and markets Chemistry.com. "Consumers are rightly making brand choices on an expanded spectrum of factors, including where a company stands on issues they care deeply about—whether that be global warming, child labor practices, partner rights for employees, or a host of other public policy matters. You don't leave your values and passions behind when you're in the checkout aisle. Meanwhile, hundreds of thousands of people have joined eHarmony, and paid them dutifully each month, without knowing where eHarmony stands and what it believes. That's simply wrong.

"[The] eHarmony [site] has been clever enough to recognize that increasingly, consumers are putting their choices under a microscope. So as the company grew into a mass-consumer brand, it began to keep their agenda quiet and cut any ties that could restrict its growth. In fact, Warren ditched his close association with Reverend Dobson and Focus on Family. In his own words, Warren admitted that the link would be a 'killer.' I'd actually have more respect for them if they didn't go through this convoluted distancing process and had the courage to stand behind Dobson. But it seems to me that Warren, seduced by Mammon in the archetypal faith versus greed struggle, decided to grow his business at the expense of his values."[3]

The question on the table: "Is that remotely possible?" Is it possible to grow a business at the expense of values? Certainly not a passion brand.

So to return to our initial question, "Why do fools fall in

love?" it's because they share a worldview. "You're my type," we say, or "you're not my type." Before we can fall in love—with a person or a brand—we need to be able to sort the prospects into "types." Brands with a clear-eyed vision of the world and where they sit in it allow us to take that initial step into potent emotional connection.

Indeed, the promise from Chemistry.com is clear: "We vow to help you find the kind of diverse, passionate people who make you go weak in the knees."

We all have our own candidates for passion brands, but surely up on many people's short list would be the energy drink Red Bull, or perhaps the Red Bull of our memories, before it started getting stacked five cartons high at the local drugstore chain. Red Bull is that funky-tasting canned beverage that will "give you wings," according to the slogans emblazed on its virtually ubiquitous delivery trucks. How does it do that? Well, it's undoubtedly in the mix of caffeine, glucose, sucrose, taurine, and glucuronolactone. It packs a wallop, albeit a short-term one with an energy free fall coming pretty quickly afterward.

According to Norbert Kraihamer, the brand's director of group marketing and sales, "Red Bull did not define a specific demographic segment as its target market: We have only people who are mentally fatigued, physically fatigued, or both."

Well, that takes most of us into account. This is marketing by inclusion, rather than the exclusionary target (women, eighteen to thirty-four) generations of marketers have favored. Red Bull took its personality to the marketplace and ended up being the drink of choice for students, drivers, clubbers, businesspeople, and sports people. How better to appeal simultaneously to these five distinct groups?

The notion of an energy drink originated in Thailand, but its global popularity can easily be credited to Dietrich

Mateschitz, a former Procter & Gamble marketing manager. He launched it in his birth country, Austria, in 1987 with the slogan "Red Bull gives you wings." It took five years for it to grow beyond the Austrian borders. In another five it was available in twenty-five markets globally, claiming 200 million units in annual sales, and ready to launch in the United States. Its growth was fueled by a short list of well-executed tactics. For example, the reliance on the one-size-fits-all silver can, the disciplined TV advertising focused only on the "gives you wings" claim, and an elastic position—revitalizes body and mind—which allowed for a wide-ranging interpretation of consumption opportunities, that is, whenever the consumer needed a lift, morning, noon, or night.

"Our consumer is adult certainly," Kraihamer explains, "but attitude based, not age, race, or gender determined."[4] Note also the ability of Red Bull to span student, clubber, and businessperson all for one consumer: This became evident when students aged, got into the business world, and took Red Bull with them to the conference room. This passion brand choice communicates wordlessly who they are and what attitude and edge they bring to the table, in sharp relief to the equally emblematic coffee, tea, and bottled water catering selections the rest of us bring.

Matthew Gonzalez, corporate director of organizational development for Toyota, explained how they decided on their appeal to potential buyers of the electric hybrid the Prius when Toyota was launching this wildly successful model. "We didn't overtarget," he told me. "We knew there were shared values we needed to appeal to. It wasn't about age or stage."[5]

For Prius, the car had to appeal to three very different personalities: tree huggers, for whom it needed to be positioned as a badge of environmentalism; early adopters, for whom it had to look different from a conventional car; and the fanatically frugal, for whom it had to convincingly demonstrate its ability to protect them from ever-escalating oil prices.

The history of the adoption of new consumer electronics illustrates this multipersonality point: The VCR owed its speed of acceptance to the efficiencies of scale enabled by the first purchasers of the fifteen-hundred-dollar early models. Once there was sufficient demand, the price was consistently lowered and more and more people could join the in-home entertainment-on-demand revolution. But who made up those early targets? Businesses and schools, which used VCRs for training and education; purchasers from high-income households, particularly those who loved new gadgets; and people who wanted to watch pornography.

This ability of brands to appeal to a powerful consumer value has been established compellingly by Richard Florida in his on-going work about the creative class. He terms it a "values-based segmentation." This type of division separates groups of consumers using "what they are paid to do" as the chief differentiator. "The creative class, all 38 million of them (30 percent of all employed people), are paid to *create the plan*," as he explains it in his book *The Rise of the Creative Class*. "The working class and the service class are paid to execute the plan."[6]

It is this creative class, then, whose members seek to badge themselves with brands that telegraph autonomy and flexibility—such as Red Bull or Prius. They demand brands that share their values, and one of these values is that they seek and enjoy innovation. What values does Florida ascribe to them? The alliterative trifecta of talent, technology, and tolerance. (Sounds like a description of Chemistry.com, too, doesn't it?)

Now, it's tempting to define these folks as the sole target worth pursuing, but, of course, that's not the point I'm making. It's not that there are right values and wrong values, but rather that passion is forged through *shared* values. Creative class workers may be forward-looking, wired, urban, and erudite, but they are also fickle, moving relentlessly and restlessly on to the next cool thing.

A great deal has been written about this deconstruction of the marketplace, using the term *postmodern marketing*. An apt illustration of its effect comes to mind when we think about the old-school target segmentation, namely, women eighteen to thirty-four, or adults ages fifty and up, or current users of competitive products. "It's not just a fragmentation of our society into numerous groups and segments, it's about the fragmentation of one consumer into a multitude of personalities," according to the Marketing Geek blog.[7]

So in one day I can search endlessly on the Web to find a leather restorer who can bring my leather wrist wallet back to life, at any price, while searching for the best deal for airline tickets. I eat lunch at a neighborhood coffee shop and dinner at Bouley, also a neighborhood eatery, albeit a four-star one. I grab close-out shampoo at Duane Reade and order a specific varietal of Elizabeth Arden mousse foundation from Lord & Taylor. I may be unwilling to drink a coffee other than Peet's at home, but settle happily for Starbucks or any other cuppa when I'm out and about.

Stephen Brown, writing in the *Journal of Marketing Management*, states the case afresh:

> Unfailingly fast, furious, frenetic, frenzied, fleeting and fragmented. It is akin to . . . shopping on speed. This disjointedness is partially attributable to the activities of marketers themselves, with their ceaseless proliferation of products, ever burgeoning channels of distribution, [and] increasingly compressed commercial breaks. It's also a response to the disconnected postmodern lifestyles, behaviors, moods, whims and vagaries of contemporary consumers. A product

of profusion with a profusion of products, the postmodern consumer performs a host of roles, each with its requisite brand name array—wife and mother, career woman, sports enthusiast, fashion victim, culture vulture, hapless holiday-maker, web surfing Internet avatar. Postmodern identities are fluid . . . postmodern personae are proliferating. An off-the-shelf self is available in your favorite styles, colors, designs, fits, and price points. Made to measure selves cost extra.[8]

One size doesn't fit all. One approach to branding won't work either. My mind-set changes. I'm not just a luxury shopper; I'm also a value-conscious shopper. I'm not just a ser-vice-oriented shopper; I'm also a convenience-driven shopper. I'm not just loyal; I'm experiential. When marketers talk about a "segment of one" marketing philosophy, they ignore that the one isn't the same in every category or every day.

Working-class and service-class groups badge themselves as well, make no mistake about it. When we conducted the quanti-tative survey, I was intrigued by several findings. First, among these working and services classes, big old brands came up as ones they felt passionate about. Folgers coffee appeared as often as Starbucks, but much more so than Maxwell House. Relatively tiny Peet's, however, breeds a cultlike commitment and adoration far beyond its market share, marketing budget, or airport-based footprint among the creative class. It's a minuscule player in the scheme of huge coffee juggernauts as read by advertising expen-ditures, sales, brand awareness or any megabrand footprint, but the love it inspires among its devotees is disproportionate and fully the equal of its Goliath-sized competitors.

So when passion brands emerge as unifiers rather than as differentiators, they become all that much more powerful. In this phase of the research, one "worldview" brand shot to the top of the list: NASCAR. It boasts tremendous enthusiasm, evangelism, self-branding, and identification with the drivers. Real NASCAR fans are rabid, not just traveling to races but organizing vacations, family reunions, and long, arduous road trips just to "be there" with their driver of choice. There's a tremendous sense of "knowing" the drivers, of understanding them that vaults above the mere celebrity gossip of movie and television stars. These drivers become family, and woe to the "real" family members who don't share the love. With that level of passion comes a corresponding consuming passion to spend leisure time and money on NASCAR and through NASCAR to support with nearly equal joy the corporate sponsors. Examples abound of family feuds over whether or not to serve Folgers or use Tide based on the commitment to the NASCAR teams these brands sponsored. "I just don't talk to them anymore," explained one NASCAR devotee about the fissure in the fabric of his family over Folgers.

With some of the brands we're most passionate about, the passion can be love or hate. Starbucks has nearly as many haters as lovers, but few coffee drinkers of any stripe are ambivalent about this category-changing brand.

Another example of mind-set marketing is the tough love of Crunch gyms. DiMassimo Goldstein's team of marketers cultivated for longtime client Crunch Fitness a campaign that demonstrates the many powerful examples of emotional benefits versus a traditional, functional series of specific performance claims anchored to key demographics.

Crunch Fitness was founded by investment banker turned stand-up comic turned aerobics studio entrepreneur Doug Levine in 1989. At first, it was just one location on St. Mark's Place in Manhattan's East Village, a tiny basement studio with faulty air-conditioning and no locker room. But from the beginning, Crunch found ways to attract a different sort of crowd from among the earnest drones who view exercise as a repetitive grind and live out "no pain, no gain" existences. In fact, part of Crunch's success centers around alienating just the sort of people who would value the comfort of reliable air-conditioning and a nice locker room over an utterly entertaining adventure.

Years later, if a sauna was broken, Levine and his managers might delay fixing it for a while. This would encourage the sort of people who weren't exactly "Crunch" to move on to other gyms. Like weeding a garden or pruning a shrub, this only encouraged the phenomenal growth of Crunch from that tiny aerobics studio to thirty-two state-of-the-art gyms in New York, Los Angeles, San Francisco, Miami, Chicago, Washington, DC, and Atlanta along with a host of popular Crunch products.

Crunch knew its customer. Levine had seen too many "hot spot" gyms head south along with the midsections of their aging membership, who were kept happy and kept paying year after year with increasingly expensive services and amenities. Ultimately these gyms lost their cool, their profitability, and their appeal to the psychodemographic, "just gotta do it better" group that makes up most prospective gym members. Levine knew that to win he'd have to *reduce* the lifetime value of a member by shortening that membership lifetime to roughly the prime gym floor—and locker room—viewing years, and then gently outsourcing the member to home exercise or a less interesting gym.

In attracting Crunch's true audience, if Levine and DiMassimo simultaneously could alienate the not-Crunch audience, the perfect formula would have been invented. So who was Crunch's true audience? He or she had moved to an urban area for a more exciting life, full of adventure and possibility. After a long day of work, the Cruncher views the gym as an *entertainment* choice. "Do I go to a club, go to the gym, or go home and watch TV and go online?"

The competition for Crunch was never seen as other gyms.

The competition consisted of other forms of *entertainment*. The Cruncher wanted entertainment that was active, adventurous, sexy, exotic, with a bit of an unpredictable anything-can-happen tint to it. The gym at Crunch was a set; the employees and members were the cast; and the exercise classes, options, and events were *programming*.

Crunch took the trouble to cast the best performers in the fitness business. Programming included everything from Hip Hop Aerobics with a live rapper, to Coed Action Wrestling, to Striptease Aerobics led by an experienced professional. Fitness instructors included drag queens, rappers, dancers, more-exotic dancers, actors, and professional athletes.

Crunch became the MTV of gyms, a *network* that knew what its audience would love and that went all out to invent, recruit, produce, and promote it. It's an interesting turn of phrase: network. Brand as network is an extremely exciting proposition for something that is typically touted for its location, hours, or equipment. Medium becoming message may be old news for networks, magazines, and other media, but for a gym to embrace the ethic is a bracing study in the art of the impossible.

The Wharton School of Business teaches a case about the problems faced by the various television networks at various times. The issue is often that they see themselves as in the "entertainment" or "news" business, but they are actually in the audience delivery business. Entertainment and news are the strategies, but the objective is ever-increasing ratings for which they can charge higher fees for advertising and programming. Follow the money. A broadcast network isn't paid by the viewers. It's paid for by advertisers who want to reach audiences.

Savvy brands seem to get that. They are the network, creating brand entertainment and news. In this model, we are the advertisers, using the brand to reach audiences (friends, family, the cute stranger across the bar) who are relevant to us.

WHAT WE TALK ABOUT WHEN WE TALK ABOUT BRANDS

Work the Worldview

Verbatim Consumer Quotes

"I'm not like anyone else, but I do love the Beatles. I do love Sam's Club. I do love my cocktail hour. I get home from work—I work two jobs—and when the kids are down and I can go out on the back deck and turn on the stereo kind of low and kick back with a Jack Daniel's, I'm home free."

"I remember wanting to have store-bought cookies, like Oreo's. Not the homemade stuff. I saw other kids had them, but my mother made 'cookies from scratch,' she called it. But I wanted Oreos. One day my mom got some for me and my sister and we sat down in front of the TV set and watched television and the commercial came on—and it was kids eating and dunking and pulling apart an Oreo, doing just what we were doing and I thought my life was perfect. My sister and I were just laughing and laughing. We belonged. To this day, I love opening packages of Oreos. I love things like that, things you can buy already and that you've seen on television. I don't like making things. Who has the time?"

"I can't be bothered. If you can't get it online, I don't need it. Who has time to shop, to go to the mall, to drive around and do those kinds of chores? There are things I'd rather be doing, lots of things besides shopping."

"It's an August day. I'd just gotten my convertible to work. It had to be repaired, but now the top could come down. My best friend and I were going to my house to pick up my stuff and then we were driving to college. It was my junior year. We were so free and had so much ahead of us. We turned on the radio and they were playing 'Classical Gas' and it just worked with the moment and the mood. We were alive and free and on the road. When I hear that music today, it takes me back there. I love that feeling, the music, the friendship, the freedom. I miss that now, in my life. Now it's all about responsibilities. But then . . ."

"I'm what you'd call conservative. I don't really like new things that much, but I do like to spend time with my family and my friends. I don't know. We just kind of sit around talking and remembering good times. We like to snack on crackers and cheese and maybe some summer sausage. That kind of thing. Just relaxing and taking it easy. It doesn't have to be special or take a long time or be gourmet; it's just us. There's food that helps us be us."

"We go all out for Christmas. I start ordering presents for the kids, my husband, our family, our friends in September. I hide them all away. It's part of the fun. Sometimes I order food things direct mail and just have them shipped, but it has to be special. Something I know they like or I think they'd like. Something that they'll open and say, 'Wow.' Something where they know I really, really thought about them."

"I've never sent a letter that required a stamp. I only do e-mail, IMing [instant messaging and texting]. That's it. If you want to reach me, it's easy."

Chapter 3
DIFFERENTIATE ON DESIGN

The moment we see and then touch an object, product, or brand, we begin to know it. Design is the first impression of that fledgling acquaintance. Is there anything more to say about incurring "gotta have it now" status other than remarking on the excellent design of the iPod? Or the iPhone? Or the MacBook Pro?

Steve Jobs, well-known founder and CEO of Apple, by all reports runs a tight design ship. The core team of designers is reputed to be about twenty in number, but nobody outside the company knows for sure, and nobody inside the company is talking. According to Daniel Turner of *Technology Review*, "Apple, Inc., has made an art of not talking about its products. Fans, journalists, and rumormongers who love it, or love to hate it, have long had to practice a sort of Kremlinology to gather the merest hints as to what is coming next out of Cupertino."[1]

In attempting to find the font of Apple greatness, all roads do seem to lead to Jobs, who Mark Rolston from Frog Design recalls even in the 1980s "wanted to elevate Apple by using

BRANDING PROCESS STEP 2

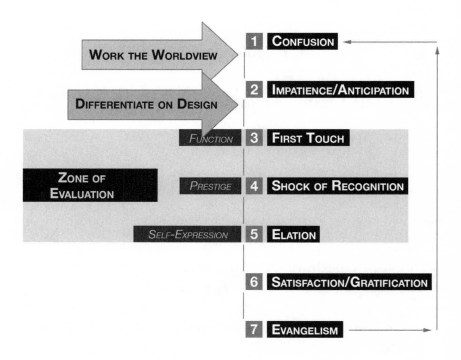

design." Essential elements of what has become the Apple world were injected early on into the genetic code of the brand. Working with Frog Design, Jobs created the "Snow White" design language—"the coherent visual vocabulary"— that helps us know we're dealing with related entities each time we touch something from Apple, whether phone, computer, laptop, or MP3 player.

In terms of design, Turner says, "That vocabulary featured, among other things, lines two millimeters wide and deep, spaced ten millimeters apart, to suggest precision. Case corners were rounded, but to differing degrees: if the curve at the back of a computer had a three-millimeter radius, the one at the front had a two-millimeter radius, reducing the machine's perceived size.

In addition, the rounded corners and lines echoed distinctive features of the Mac user interface of the time: rounded screen corners and horizontal lines in the grab bars of windows."

Paul Kunkel, author of *AppleDesign*, quotes a codesigner of the Apple Lisa as saying that Jobs was looking for the kind of design statement that Italian Olivetti achieved in the 1970s: "[It was] an undisputed leader in industrial design." This focus by the founder on design is tremendously crucial: "Critical to Apple's success in design is the way Jobs brought focus and discipline to the product teams."[2]

Don Norman, former vice president of advanced technology at Apple, told Turner, "The businessman wants to create something for everyone, which leads to products that are middle of the road. Jobs had a single, cohesive image of the final product and would not allow any deviation, no matter how promising a new proposed feature appeared to be. Other companies are more democratic, listening to everyone's opinions, and the result is bloat and a lack of cohesion.

"The hardest part of design, especially consumer electronics, is keeping features out. Simplicity is in itself a product differentiator and pursuing it can lead to innovation."

Another colleague, DIGO's Mark DiMassimo, puts the Jobs genius in another light: "The most fundamental thing about Apple that's interesting to me is that they are just as smart about what they *don't* do. Great products can be made more beautiful by omitting things."[3]

Why does great design help instill brand passion? There's a growing body of emotion and motivation research suggesting that small things, like well-designed products, are rewarding in and of themselves. And when we look at them, use them, and share them, it makes us happy, which leads to more creative, happier associations with the product or brand. Conversely, when things are ugly, don't work, or break, we become impatient, cranky, and frustrated. One further insight is that once computing reached beyond the office and into the home, it needed to become more lovable. As designer Michael Graves put it, "What can make a domestic setting truly home is the infusion of a cultural dimension." What is more of a cultural dimension in a consumer culture than a delightfully designed product like Graves's iconic tea kettle or an iBook? An iPod allows us to take that domestic setting with us, literally transforming our surroundings wherever we are. It's no wonder that many iPod owners clutch it so closely.

I've done enough research in consumer electronics and particularly with digital music devices to know that the underlying emotional goal is a feeling of "synchronicity." This is the sense that both the music playing and our current activity are in sync. The music serves as a soundtrack not to someone else's movie but to our own imagined one, spooling out right now, real time, in our mind's screen. It imparts tremendous significance to the moment. When the portable music device we're using is also one with great functional performance features, simplicity, and a brand mark that has cultural resonance—an iPod, not an Onda—we're triply blessed. The generic joy of the experience is made more keen by the specific brand.

Car design is another arena in which we're prepared to be thrilled. The story of Cadillac's popularity, demise, and resurgence is one of design. I had the opportunity to work on the brand just as its demise was becoming a poorly kept secret. The canard "every time a hearse goes by means we've lost another customer" was most likely coined for Cadillac, although it's true for a wide cross-section of brands.

For generations prior to that, Cadillac had been the auto industry's gold standard, essentially the pace car for automotive innovation. It was Cadillac that had pioneered the electric self-starter in 1912, Cadillac that had introduced the V-8 engine in 1914, and Cadillac that had machined truly inter-changeable parts, making mass production a reality. Up until the 1950s it was the trendsetter for design as well. Cadillac became the culture's term for excellence, best in class.

By the 1980s, however, the brand's fortunes had dimmed perceptibly. There really is nothing harder than to turn a big, clunky brand around. The company decided what was needed was an entry-level, small luxury sedan to compete head-on with the incursions being made by Mercedes-Benz, Audi, and BMW. What it came up with was the 1982 Cimarron. The brand thought it could sell seventy-five thousand of the model in year one, at a base price of a bit over twelve thousand dol-lars. Instead, it sold a bit fewer than twenty-six thousand. Cadillac owners didn't like it because it was not at all what they wanted in a car; drivers of competitive cars didn't like it because it was built on the same platform as the Chevy Cava-lier, which cost half as much. So the brand started over, aban-doning the Cimarron totally by 1988.

In 1986 Cadillac was ready to launch the most recent result of its long-standing relationship with the legendary Italian car design firm Pininfarina, well known in the United States for its Alfa Romeo, Ferrari, and Maserati work. Three years earlier, Cadillac and Pininfarina reached an agreement for the Cadillac Allenté, a two-seater convertible. It was the first time that Gen-eral Motors had assigned the style, design, and construction of the car body to an outside firm.

The undertaking was epic: every day via an Air Bridge, cargo planes filled with Allenté bodies left Turin, Italy, headed for Detroit. More than twenty-two thousand were created until production ceased in 1993. This was a breathtakingly designed car, gorgeous to look at, spectacular to sit in, and terrific to drive. But design alone couldn't do the trick for Cadillac.

Neither could marketing alone: remember the Zig-Zag

campaign that tried to reach out to younger drivers, positioning the 1990s yuppies in an unsuccessful attempt to woo them away from their BMWs? Nope. That effort didn't do the trick either. It was not until the late '90s that Cadillac design and the zeitgeist aligned. Enter Cadillac's SUV the Escalade, which means "the act of scaling defensive walls or ramparts with the aid of ladders, and was a prominent feature of siege warfare in medieval times," according to Wikipedia. "It was one of the most direct options available for attacking a fortification, but was also one of the most dangerous."

One can't help but feel it was aptly named, given the state of the Cadillac über-brand at that point, plus the inroads of aggressive competition. Reportedly the first version went into production only ten months after approval; that's warp speed in automotive terms. But something in the way it moved, so to speak, made it work for Escalade and for the Cadillac Brand.

Perhaps it was the steroid-engorged version of the Escalade EXTm that really turbo-charged the entire company. It appeared in the popular movie *The Matrix Reloaded*, showcasing the luxury of an SUV with the functionality of a pick-up truck tricked out with sinister deep-tinted windows, ebony diamond paint with black chrome exterior, and an all–black leather interior. Go figure. "Insidiously appealing," raved PickupTrucks .com. Pretty soon the Escalade forged a major presence in pop culture, particularly hip-hop culture, which I believe provides the air cover for mere mortals to buy and drive a Cadillac of any stripe. It's not our mother's Fleetwood. It's Tony Soprano's conveyance of choice; Christopher Moltisanti's too, after the Maserati got totaled. In *Family Guy* it's termed "God's wheels."

Of course, we are used to thinking about design as one of the imperatives of big-ticket items, like great technology or fabulous cars, but we'd be wrong to give it short shift in any domain. Simplehuman is a company that has redesigned common household objects like trash cans, and made the two-hundred-dollar trash can an essential. The credo of this company, as expressed on its Web site Simplehuman.com, is as straightforward as its products: "We design housewares to make you more efficient at home—from a spoon rest on a utensil holder to a pedal that'll outlast 50,000 steps, or a paper towel holder that won't unravel and a dish rack that drains in different directions. We know we've done our job when you wonder how it's possible to love a trash can that much."

This is one company that also embraces the "brand democracy" tenet, as witnessed by its annual design competition. Last year's winning design was an in-sink dish mat, made to control dirty dish clutter. The mat sits in the sink, allowing the dishes to be organized like in a conventional dish rack, thereby preventing breakage. More important, it ensures the dishes can be rinsed without standing dirty water accumulating.

OXO is another company focused on the daily grind: "OXO is dedicated to providing innovative consumer products that make everyday living easier," reads its mission statement. We may not know how to pronounce it (Ox-Oh is preferred), but we surely know its Good Grips line of kitchen tools.

The Home Hero Fire Extinguisher, designed by the Arnell Group, is a fabulous example of the process through which great design actually makes the product function better: It's so gorgeous and available in so many fashion-forward materials, colors, and finishes that owners are loathe to put it in the out-of-the-way hiding places to which a more typical fire extinguisher is relegated. Thus, they are much more likely to be able to grab it when they need it.

The world of product design is ripe with talent, and the marketplace seems to reward and encourage exciting thinking. There's the PalmPeeler from Chef'n Corporation, making a vegetable peeler that fits into your palm, secured by a ring. There's the SmartMoney clip, developed for CitiCorp Credit Services. When it's waved near a receiver base, transactions under twenty-five dollars are processed automatically. There's the Aliph Jawbone Bluetooth Headset, packaged to make it look like a modern museum piece. Each of these examples won international design awards and they are just the tip of the iceberg.

Even consumer-friendly marketing has a design element to it. Bank of America and the design group IDEO teamed up to understand baby-boomer women with children and how they deal with banking. The pressing issue was saving money. This led Bank of America to create the Keep the Change program, through which any purchase made with a Visa debit card issued by the bank is rounded up to the nearest dollar—the difference is put in a savings account. In less than one year, 2.5 million customers became engaged by the campaign, generating 700,000 new checking accounts and 1 million new savings accounts.

So with consumers enamored of intuitive, exciting, and usable design and the proven strength of the market to reward and encourage relevant creativity, why is the world of packaged goods so bereft of great package and product design?

R.Bird & Company publishes package and product design analysis on a pretty frequent basis covering categories such as tea, breakfast cereals, coffees, women's shaving products, and more. The frequently described "shelf shock" is self-evident if you've been to the tea aisle of a grocery store recently. It's stuffed to the rafters with various color systems, claims, and packaging protocols, but trying to shop it is an exercise in frustration. One of the comments in the tea report states the case cogently: "It's astounding to see that a product with a culturally rich history can find its way to such an abhorrent end. Even a very brief study of the rich heritage of tea, its varieties, culture and rituals, leads one to recognize such insensitivity in presentations, both packaging and product."[4]

When I worked on SnackWell's for Nabisco, part of its storied heritage was "the big green wall." This refers to the green packaging for all SnackWell's products and the fact that they were merchandised together on the store shelves in vertical product facings that made a bold statement to the consumer. Part of that statement was that reduced-fat and lower-calorie cookies had been legitimized, no longer stigmatized by being shelved in dusty, little-used sections of the store. Women responded to that legitimacy cue in droves. These were good-tasting cookies, marketed like a big brand in a logical, visually coherent way, not as a niche player, as Metrecal—remember those diet wafer cookies and shakes in dusty boxes above the frozen food section in the '60s and '70s?—had been years before.

In packaged foods the stress on packaging is the functional role it must play: preserving the product safely for long shelf life while communicating the brand's name and proposition, ideally as cheaply as possible. Packaging costs are viewed as a capital equipment expense, a purchasing expense, or a commodity cost, not as an element of marketing. That is such a missed opportunity in today's marketplace.

The American market is one that responds to design, but there is little to excite us as we walk down the grocery aisles. Think of what Martha Stewart's lines have done for Kmart and now Macy's. Think of what Michael Graves's "Works of Art That Work" has done for Target shoppers. Graves was already a world-famous architect when he agreed to design modest household products for the home for Target, firm in the belief that "Good design should be accessible to all," as Target's Web site quotes him as saying. Together, the store and the man bet that people would respond to better thought-out designs for tea kettles, toasters, and blenders, and they've won that bet right along with any of us who has purchased one of those fabulous products.

Well-designed products implicitly trust the consumer to take notice. The consumer does notice, recognizing the thoughtfulness that is the hallmark of great design and reveling in the shared belief that the choice to opt for something beautiful matters. I would love to see the tea section as reimagined by a Michael Graves; I'd love to see packaged cookies redesigned by Apple-esque design teams.

The first time I worked on a packaged goods brand that differentiated itself with respect to design, I saw the power of this approach in action. The brand was Softsoap, introduced by an entrepreneur named Robert Taylor from Minnetonka, Minnesota. He stumbled on the idea of liquid hand soap in a pump dispenser and quickly realized that an idea this big would rapidly have competitors, and that the two most likely competitors, Procter & Gamble and Lever Brothers, were not to be fooled around with. They each boasted a major national sales force, sophisticated marketing power, and generations-long relationships with buyers in grocery, convenience, drug, and the then-emerging mass channels of trade.

How does a tiny start-up company attempt to compete? With design. Taylor made a game-changing bet: He could not patent-protect his brainchild; liquid soap had been a public washroom staple for years, after all. But he knew that the toughest part of the consumer product–manufacturing process was getting the pumps to work and only two companies made the pumps. He placed an order for one million pumps—a year-and-a-half supply—thereby locking out competition for that window of time. It was long enough to build a savvy marketing campaign and a distributor sales force of his own. Ultimately, he sold the brand to Unilever, which found it was better to pay for the consumer passion Softsoap had earned than to try replicating it.

WHAT WE TALK ABOUT WHEN WE TALK ABOUT BRANDS

Differentiate on Design

Verbatim Consumer Quotes

"I just wanted to touch it. It seemed so cool. It was a Nokia phone, silver. It seemed like it could connect me to the world and help the world understand who I was. I thought I'd be James Bond if I had that phone."

"The way the Pringles canister just held them all so neat. I loved that. My mom would let me eat Pringles in my room because the lid sealed them in tight and she didn't have to worry about bugs and stuff. That's all we'd ever ask for. Just Pringles and we could have them in our rooms and they weren't greasy, so we could work on the computer and not get the keyboard all greasy. I was a geek and stuff like that mattered. Pringles were for people like me. Not big loud party Lays, but quiet, neat, techno-geeky."

"It was a four-hundred-dollar coffee maker. A KitchenAid, but once I saw it, I really couldn't settle for anything else. It was just so beautiful. I made due with an old French press from my mother until I saved up enough to get it. It was so beautiful and you could put it on automatic and you'd wake up to the smell of coffee in the morning. There was just nothing like it. It was four hundred dollars, can you imagine?"

"I was in the fifth grade and I saw a pair of Walt Clyde Frazier shoes and I wanted them. I just begged and begged for them. Finally, I got them. I saved up and I got them and they were terrible. Just terrible shoes. I put them under my bed so my mother wouldn't see and remember I wasn't wearing them and I put my Converse sneakers back on and that was it. I never strayed again."

"I was at the gym and I saw someone with these earbuds on. Earbuds—I know now that's what they're called, but then I just stared. I hadn't seen them before, and then I saw that it was connected to something, which turned out to be an iPod. Suddenly, it seemed that everywhere I looked, people had these things in their ears connected to this little iPod thingy. It was like it happened overnight and I wanted to be one of those people. I struck up a conversation with a stranger at the gym and listened to it and it was amazing and I just had to have it. It wasn't about price or anything. I just had to have it."

"I got this Williams-Sonoma catalog and I hadn't heard of it before. Then, before long I saw a Williams-Sonoma store at the mall and I thought I'd go in. They were sampling something, some kind of peach pound cake or something and you could buy the mix and it was so good. I just wandered around, nibbling on a couple of pieces of the pound cake and then I saw these little kitchen tools, like to scrub pans with and to open cans with and they looked so cute and modern and not like anything I'd seen. They were only like five or six dollars each or something, so I got them. I still have them. They work great. Black and kind of industrial cool looking."

Chapter 4
HIRE PASSIONISTAS

Passion brands breed passionate followings, very often through impassioned employees. I remember the early stories of Red Bull, when dogged sales guys would bring empty cans to bars and leave them crunched up and strewn around to make the brand look like it was popular, well before it actually was. Contemplate the likelihood of that happening with the launch of a new diet cola or cereal bar.

If the brand stewards think of the brand they work on as an interchangeable part in the cogs of their careers, then they also become interchangeable parts in the cogs of the brand's career. This codependency is what often happens as a brand makes the move from cult to common, but it is not the same as passion.

Early in my career, I worked on the launch of a new version of an old household favorite: Crest. We were launching Tartar Control Formula Crest. The assistant brand manager looked me in the eye at one point and explained: "Your job isn't to sell more Crest. Your job is to ensure that I become the

BRANDING PROCESS STEP 3

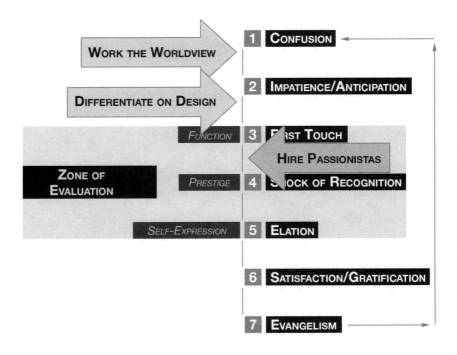

youngest brand manager in Procter & Gamble's history. If you do that, you'll also be selling more Crest, I'm sure. You'll also be gaining credentials for your own career. But keep your eye on the prize. The prize is my career."

This is a true story. What came next is also true. That assistant achieved her goal. Then she left the company, got her MBA at Harvard, became the steward of a storied though now deceased automotive mark, left to be swept up and down in the dot-com boom and bust, before being recruited to become head of an ad agency. Her career has thrived—and so has Crest's—but each was simply a way station for the other.

The world of consumer packaged goods—the world of Crest, Tide, Bounce, Secret, and scores of other household brands—is the world most often of commodities, the "stack 'em high and sell 'em low" world of modern grocery and club store retailing. It is often the purview of careerists relentlessly moving onward every three years, up or out of the corporate food chain. Corporate secrets and competitor espionage are the rule, because the culture is often one of brand warfare. It is rarely the world of brand passion.

The world of genuine brand passion is much different. There are four common denominators among diverse passion brands. I summarize them in the next paragraphs, but the case studies in this chapter illustrate these points clearly. Passion brands attract and invigorate passionate people, inside the company as much as outside.

First, the people working in these industries also play in them: they spend their leisure time pursuing an understanding of their work-a-day world. Their vocations and their avocations have become one.

Second, there is a genuine lack of an adversarial vision. As one person told me about competition in an industry: "One hand washes the other; both hands wash the face." It is fair to state that passion brands are often the earliest entrants or pioneers in their categories. Red Bull forged the energy drink business; iPod created its category; Specialized Bicycle Components launched the mountain biking revolution with its StumpJumper model. The "first player" position makes it important to grow the category, not just a brand. Otherwise, an exciting new idea can founder and fail as one company attempts to create and dominate its market.

Third, as a result, passion brands use different metrics from the ubiquitous market share of the packaged goods world. They do not see the market as stagnant, a fixed pie, in which my brand's growth can only come at the expense of your brand's sales. Instead, they focus on creating and building their category, on mission and purpose—and success is often signaled by the accolades of knowledgeable peers, such as journalists or restaurateurs in the case of food and wine, by buzz from fans, by the sight of people willing to wait all night outside for the new release, be it wine, music, a movie, or an iPhone.

Fourth, there is a lifeblood in passion brands that makes them move, change, and evolve. A specific idea may not work, but it's seen as a stepping stone to something that ultimately may, rather than the X on the forehead of a once-promising careerist. Passion brands are forgiving of mistakes by the people who work on them. Indeed, they seem to come from companies and people who encourage the trials that lead to error, accepting failure as the table stakes in the game that is played for eventual success.

Thus passion brands are not static but living, capable of making great progress—and of making mistakes. Martha Stewart comes to mind. Look at all the ways she and her colleagues have grown her "brand" from a book about weddings from a Connecticut caterer. She has tried many approaches along the way to becoming a major media company, with the occasional well-documented stumbles.

From such enthusiasm can come great leaps forward and some major missteps, but the culture of the company is forgiving and the passionate consumer, perhaps intuiting this, embraces the company perspective and becomes forgiving as well. Acceptance of a mistake becomes a mark of brand belonging. Stewart's tumble into prison was remarkable both for the fact that it happened and because her audience forgave her so quickly.

On some level, passion brands are elite brands. They are not for everybody and they don't try to be, in terms of whom they employ, what they make, and which customers they seek. Employing passionistas means skipping over plenty of perfectly capable workers who just aren't that excited. Passion brands may often be products that are limited by availability, price, and perception of value. In this rarefied climate, the products send forth cues as subtle as dog whistles, cues that few consumers can hear. But those who do are rewarded by a welcoming sense of kinship, not solely by the brand but by its makers. The term I used to describe the very tip of the passion brand pyramid (see figure on page 90) is "World-Class Elite."

The best example I've come across of this productive elitism is Specialized Bicycle Components. Its founder, president, and inspiration is Mike Sinyard, and I know from experience he'd rather go for a ride every day in the hills around Mountain View, California, with his equally fanatical colleagues than discuss marketing.

He rides every day. They all do. These are professional-level riders. At least part of the kick they get out of it is that it's their job. They are just thrilled that they get to make money and spend their workday doing what they'd more than likely be spending money on and doing with their leisure time: riding, thinking, obsessing, and talking about biking. That is where great passion brands derive their fuel: people who work there would be fixated on the product whether they are paid to be or not.

Another fitness focused brand, Title 9 Sports, benefits equally from the passion of its founder and the engagement such passion brings with the consumer. Missy Park started the company after not being able to find a well-fitting jogging bra in a classic sports store. She was irritated as well by the smirks and unease of the predominantly male sales staff. Her hands-on approach and recruitment of others who share her zealous love of fitness and the clothing that enables it is legendary. Still, it's Missy's voice that brands the Title 9 catalog, Web site, and retail locations as places for passionistas.

"Look, we sell clothes, sports clothes, fitness and yoga

clothes, but at the end of the day, it's just apparel, it's the rag trade," she explains to me. "What gets me out of bed in the morning is the transformative power of sport. Getting girls and women to participate in sports and fitness is really what we at Title 9 are about."

Moving to another industry, the Mondavi winery and, thanks largely to Robert Mondavi, most of California's wines, are further illustrations of products fueled by the passion of their creators. In order to appreciate what he did, we have to recall how wines were marketed in the middle part of the twentieth century in America: cheap gallons of Napa Valley varietals, or imports "branded" for the presumed ignorant consumers who couldn't be trusted to pronounce the names, understand the label intricacies, or appreciate the sophisticated tastes of authentic French, German, or Italian wines. Thus, words like "Hearty Burgundy," Mateus, Lancer's, and Blue Nun took hold, ultimately to become terms of derision.

As Robert Mondavi wrote in his autobiography, *Harvests of Joy: How the Good Life Became Great Business*, "I knew we could become one of the great wine-producing regions of the world. But the American wine industry was still in its infancy and no one seemed to have the knowledge, the vision, or the guts to reach for the gold, to make wines that could stand proudly next to the very best from France, Germany and Spain."[1]

The curator of the Napa Valley Museum told me that American wines emerged with three "shots heard round the world": first, the 1976 Bicentennial Tasting in Paris; second, the Baron Philippe and Bob Mondavi Opus One partnership; and third, the *60 Minutes* story on the "French Paradox." The paradox, first reported more than a decade ago, is that the French seemingly eat and drink all the wrong things by American dietary standards and yet lead happy, healthy lives. Their secret: drinking red wine daily.

As Nina Weims of the Robert Mondavi winery explained to me, "Robert was the first one to understand that American wine had to be put on a level playing field with art, music, and gastronomy. He understood it could be a taste acquired along with other aspirational tastes. He brought the pioneering chef and restaurateur Alice Waters here. He created the Culinary Institute here."[2] He did many other things right, including entering a California wine in a French Bordeaux tasting in 1976 and winning.

Another of those right steps was the partnership with Baron Philippe de Rothschild to create Opus One. The Rothschilds had been producing wines since 1853 when Baron Nathaniel de Rothschild took possession of the Chateau Mouton Estate in Bordeaux. Robert Mondavi founded his in Napa Valley in 1966. The idea was to connect the Rothschild's pedigree and prominence within the wine world to raise the reputation of California and specifically Mondavi wines.

According to contemporaneous reports, this legendary union was all done on a handshake in just about two hours. It seems to have served as the model for every Mondavi venture that followed. "Ours was an accord built on shared passions and mutual trust," Mondavi wrote in his autobiography. "And not once . . . did the Baron ever change one iota of our initial agreement, nor did he waver from our initial goals and spirit."

Nina Weims had explained that Mondavi had a great aesthetic sensibility, but nothing quite prepares the visitor for the vision of the Opus One winery. An article in the *Wine Spectator* described it: "First you descend a stately spiral staircase that opens onto a dimly lit hallway. At the end of the hall is a tasting room with a dramatic curved glass wall that overlooks a sweeping semicircular vista—to your right and left, rows of barrels stretch away into obscurity. The effect is breathtaking."[3] The total cost of construction for the thirty-thousand-barrel-per-year facility was $26.5 million, an amount impossible to recoup quickly, even with a bottle going for $150 at the winery, $250 in retail stores, and upward of $300 in restaurants.

The vice president of sales makes the passion brand point about the importance of scarcity as well as commitment: "Here at Opus One, we're making the best wine we know how to. We can only make thirty thousand cases and it's all sold before we've bottled it. All the bean counters laughed at the baron and Mondavi, but it was the baron and Mondavi who were right: We're on allocation continuously at $150 a bottle—at the winery. Only a very few can get it." Now that's world-class elite.

So why make it? For the same reason that Ralph Lauren makes purple and black label suits: The brands may or may not be profitable, but their main purpose is to lend respect and value to the entire family of products under them. The wine consumer, it was trusted, would know that Mondavi's less-expensive wines benefited from the same growing regions and management as Opus One. The upper reaches of the brand's halo confer presumed delights to any product nestled within.

Mondavi's story also illustrates the passion brand's characteristic (lack of adversarialism) and its focus on creating a category rather than grabbing market share. Mondavi opened the door to fine American wine not only for himself, but for his northern California colleagues to walk through with him. And his ethos is widespread. When I first started working in the industry for Korbel Champagnes and Brandy, I was shocked to find that one of my first days visiting the winery would be spent traveling to meet all the other winemakers in the area so I could taste their offerings and talk with them about Korbel's.

The marketing director of the Hess Collection of wines later summed up the redefinition of competition to me like this: "The success of Opus One was a triumph for all of us. It raised the bar and the price ceiling for all of us. We all benefit from quality improvement. We share our advances with each other, so that the entire valley benefits."[4]

The sales manager at Schramsberg Vineyards put this collegiality in a more specific context when I spoke with him. "When our corker broke and we were six months away from having a new one, I called the winery down the hill and they made a shift on their champagne line available to us. We just had to pay their workers. We know we're all in this together."[5]

Imagine for a moment Colgate calling Crest to say, "Our capper broke. Can we use one of your lines to make our product?"

The sense that we're all in it together means everyone works toward the goal of a great vintage. In the world of packaged goods, the marketers are often in the home office, sales is spread apart and works various territories, and manufacturing is in multiple locations throughout the country. Each discipline is its own fiefdom. In these elite passion brand settings, there's no distance when it counts. "We're right here: offices, production, bottling, everything in sight of the vineyards," Hess explains to me during our meeting. "If it's not in the grape, it won't be in the bottle. Being here is how we stay focused. You can't do this long distance."[6]

A worker at Artesa vineyard clarifies this point further, when I ask about the company's ethos: "When the moment for the harvest comes, the vineyard master knows it. Then it's all hands on deck. They've called in all the office workers to be in the fields on Saturdays, if we're short-handed. I've worked the fields; so has my boss and my boss's boss."[7]

As Gary Heck, head of Korbel, put it years ago when I worked on this brand and we discussed the remarkable collegiality in the wine industry, "We drink each other's wines. We enjoy each other's triumphs. There's enough success to go around."[8] How do competitors till these fields in such harmony? There are a couple of noncontradictory hypotheses.

One is that so much of a product like wine is out of any single maker's control. "Have the humility to listen to what the soil is telling you," as Peter Sichel, the legendary, now deceased winery owner and wine importer told me when I worked with him for the German Wine Academy. Patricia Palermo, former marketing director of Domaine Chandon, told me, "It's the romance of the endless unknowns of wine, the heroism of the hope, the promise of the product, the next vintage that draws people here and keeps them here. They may arrive as tourists, but the dream is to return and live on the land."[9]

The marketing director of Schramsberg puts it in different but equally poetic language: "We are a fragile, agricultural product. Everything matters: the soil, the light, the moisture, the heat, *when* each comes, how much, how often. Everything makes a difference in the size and quality of the harvest and therefore of the wine."[10]

This fragility is an element that in most manufacturing processes is persistently reduced as much as possible through formulas, automation, and other efforts to winnow out chance, mistakes, and deviation from the mean. Understandably so: one wants to know that the Crest one buys at the airport in a panic will have the familiar taste, feel, touch, and benefits as the tube mistakenly left at home. But a level of risk and unpredictability allows for personal involvement and therefore passion. Being able to make a difference in the ultimate product enjoyment gives wine part of its panache and its passion. Get it now, before it's gone.

The wine business is the kind of industry where you can't fake it. It requires an obsessive attention to detail and love of the craft in the doing of it, not just the selling. So, too, with sports equipment, like Specialized Bicycle Components, and with high-end fashion, where a designer's wit, skill, and a raw joy in how a certain fabric will drape itself on the body coalesce to change how we dress. The same is true of great travel destinations, like the Amanresorts with their personal and pervasive anticipation of desires, which guests don't know they have until they are met. The experience seems custom-made, created by people who love what they are doing, for people who are ready, willing, and able to appreciate it. There's an inherent belief that nothing will be lost on the audience, which conveys a tremendous respect.

Another industry that seems a magnet for passionistas is fine dining. As Phoebe Damrosch writes in *Service Included*, her memoir of working at fabled Per Se in Manhattan, every worker in the restaurant is referred to as chef. She quotes the meta-chef Thomas Keller as explaining to the staff the difference between involvement and commitment: "If you want to understand commitment . . . look at the American breakfast of bacon and eggs. The chicken was involved, but the pig was committed."[11]

Fresh Direct illustrates the power of commitment in terms of whom they hire. They don't just sell bread; they have a baker who developed parbaked breads to be finished at home, which is reportedly the only way to ensure that the consumer gets the texture and taste of fresh-baked bread. Is it? Or is it comparable to the old Duncan Hines recipe: When they introduced packaged cake mixes, they could have used powered eggs, but they believed the homemaker would want to contribute "something" essential in the process, so they asked her to add the egg.

I don't know if parbaking is essential, but I do know that it makes for some scrumptious breads, all amazingly aromatic and fresh. Among the offerings: black olive, raisin pecan, rose-mary ciabatta, focaccia, challah, jalapeno cornbread, semolina-seeded demi-baguette, parmesan bâtarde, round brioche, wheat nut bâtarde.

The cheeses at Fresh Direct are another revelatory and gustatory delight, and the credit is due this time to Ken Blanchette, cheesemonger, or as he's described on the site, "our fab fromager." Cypress Grove Chèvre, Purple Haze, Coach Farm black pepper low-fat goat cheese stick, Greek feta, Artisanal Reny Picot Selection Camembert, Les Folies Fromages white fig fruit spread for goat cheeses. It's endless.

None of this seems precious, not even the profiles of the various department managers, which include their favorite quotes. David Weber, the master butcher, quotes Orson Welles: "My doctor told me to stop having intimate dinners for four. Unless there are three other people." He also describes his career in terms designed to make us eager to order: "I made it my business to know everything about meat. I'm self-taught, a survivor, and a perfectionist—these qualities, plus a standard of excellence, result in a high-quality product."[12]

Weber is obviously a passionista who has been in the industry for more than thirty years, selling to upscale, world-renowned restaurants like Peter Lugar's Steakhouse in Brooklyn and specialty markets like Stew Leonard's in Connecticut. It's by attracting and keeping him and his colleagues that Fresh Direct has grown as it has, not just geographically throughout New York City but also through the depth and range of offerings. Beyond the delivery of groceries, it's developed quick meal solutions from restaurants throughout the city, including Rosa Mexicano and Chef Terrance Brennan, the creative genius behind restaurants like Artisanal and Picholine in New York.

Just as passion brands are more than the darlings of "early adopters," they can also become more than boutique brands.

Let's never forget that Hellmann's Mayonnaise is on this list. The temptation, of course, is to view them as elitist, and certainly the foodie who categorically states she could never even date someone who uses Miracle Whip is an elitist despite the fact that Hellmann's is a common grocery store brand.

Stephen Brown put it this way in a rapid-fire series of e-mails we engaged in as I sought to clarify the micro vs. macro issue and its application to passion brands: "I suspect, in fact, that small, seemingly exclusive, cult brands would be especially prone to passionate support, support they are liable to lose as the brand becomes bigger and more mainstream. Innocent Drinks (a brand of fruit smoothies and juices sold throughout the United Kingdom), for example. There is a negative side to consumer passion: conservatism. Brand fans are very protective of their 'property' and they don't like to see it change. This can make life difficult for brand managers when it's time to refresh."[13]

Thus, the passionate love of a brand can be constricting by its very nature. The thing we adore about it must not be changed, and yet change is exactly what keeps the brand fresh. It creates a dichotomy that is perpetually vexing to big companies that acquire passion brands in the hopes of continuing their early-growth curves.

Here's the model I've used to illustrate the ways in which passion brands expand (when they can). They can reach large numbers of consumers, not by moving away from the powerful particularity of World-Class Elitism, but rather by creating a series of stepping stones through which consumers can gain as much of a toehold to that world as they desire.

As a company expands beyond the tip of the pyramid, it moves to the second tier, the Enthusiast Company. This is where I'd put an Oakley eyewear or Converse high-tops. Here the brand loosens its limits on availability but still says some-

PASSION BRAND PYRAMID

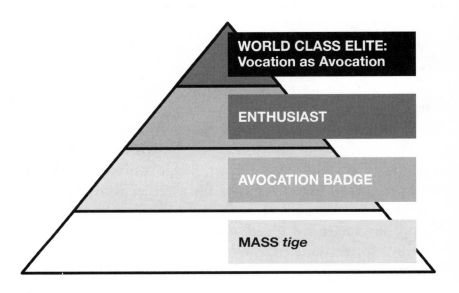

thing extra about the consumer. The brand functions as a mark of belonging in the world of the brand—even if you're not a member of a cycling or skiing team, you can look like one. It becomes a way for consumers to say something about themselves. That "something" begins the badging effect of using a brand to tell others about themselves. Brands in this category are helping us demonstrate where we spend our leisure time and money.

My own favorite coffee company (although I so very much respect the ethics and passion of Starbucks) is Peet's. Why? Because I know it's not a brand that is jealous of Starbucks, but is rather doing its own thing, based on its own heritage and belief system, which it has bothered to share with me. I went to Peet's first in Berkeley, California, on a business trip. I learned it's a northern California legend run by the iconoclastic Alfred Peet, who Starbucks CEO and founder Howard

Schultz says, "treats coffee like wine, appraising it in terms of origins and estates and years and harvests."[14]

Alfred Peet apparently was inspired by his father, a roaster in the Netherlands. Peet arrived in San Francisco in the 1950s, working for a coffee-importing company that supplied beans to Hills Brothers and Folgers. "I couldn't understand why in the richest country in the world they were drinking such poor-quality coffee," Peet told Mark Pendergrast, author of *Uncommon Grounds: The History of Coffee and How It Transformed Our World.* By 1966 he was ready to solve that quandary, opening its store in Berkeley and showing the world how a great bean should be roasted, ground, and brewed. The word spread. He inspired others. Indeed, three partners started Starbucks Coffee, Tea, and Spice at Pike's Place Market in Seattle based on a belief in what Peet's was doing at Berkeley. Other cities started their own versions of Peet's in Denver, San Diego, and Pittsburgh, attracting an enthusiastic band of regulars who brought friends and family. It was the equivalent of the rise of the microbreweries.[15]

I remember trying to convince a fellow at Peet's to send me ground coffee or even beans for me to grind myself. He was adamant that I needed to use the beans the day they were roasted. He wouldn't do it. Nothing like turning away a customer to make them want you. I begged. I called the shop when I thought he might not be there and thought I could wheedle a separate deal with someone else. But no. Finally, I guess, Peet's decided that shipping standards were now up to his standards and I get a shipment every month. Phew. A pure enthusiast brand.

A bit farther down the pyramid we see the emergence of "Badge Avocation" status. In this level, the brand is the aspiration, not the activity or pursuit it represents. I really don't need high-performance gear in order to drive to Home Depot over the weekend, but an off-road vehicle just completes my look, for example. All the technical features of the SUV are marketed as if they were designed by those who love outdoor adventure; but for most, the fancy features are never used. Maybe once a year the thing gets put into four-wheel drive, but it's always a nerve-wracking decision to try it. What has been purchased is the dream of escape, of exploits, of the roads not taken.

As you see, the model gets wider at the bottom, appealing to more and more people in its aspirational intent, while at once more general, useful for more occasions and contexts. This is the world that major marketers dream of inhabiting, a vast entry portal corroborated by layers of credibility above.

There are brands that compete at all of these levels: Think about the purple-labeled Ralph Lauren line and then watch it move down through RL to Ralph to the versions launched at JCPenney's in 2008 without his name attached, but with his approach to lifestyle apparel unharmed. Donna Karan has done similar laddering with her fashion marks. Automobile brands do this all the time: You enter the Mercedes world at various levels of luxury; BMW with its 3, 4, 5, 6, 7-series makes it particularly simple to follow where on the pyramid you're entering. So does price, of course.

It is in the top three tiers of brands where peer review, whether in conventional media or on the Web, matters most. Passion brands in these three echelons have dedicated journalists who track them: *Wine Enthusiast* with its now well-known ranking systems and *Cigar Aficionado* with its equivalent point system (both magazines are from Marvin Shanken) are just two, but for films, books, theater, opera, ballet, mountain bikes, travel, fashion, and scores of other lifestyle pursuits there are dedicated trade and enthusiast publications galore. Not so for toothpaste or more everyday packaged goods.

Positive reviews can make or break passion brands. This

becomes an essential element of the business model—the passion must be communicated to and through the cognoscenti, the experts. We know about fashion shows and fashion magazines. We read about movie junkets, previews, and press tours. There are massive national and international trade shows for other industries such as sporting goods and consumer electronics that acknowledge the three-way collaboration among maker, writer, and user. In the wine industry, this is so much the case that one journalist tells me, "The cost of creating a winery from the ground up must now include a $250,000 'cottage' for visiting wine writers who've come to expect to be treasured guests."

Another powerful example of passionate employees is Amanresorts, which, since its inception in 1988 with Amanpuri on the northwest coast of Phuket (the biggest island in Thailand, located in the Andaman Sea), has set the bar as the elite respite for world-weary travelers. One manager promoted over the years from a waitress position told *Destination* magazine reporter Cynthia Rosenfeld, "It's about conveying a warm, family feeling so that the guest is not just a hotel guest but like someone staying at a friend's home. Our guests have become like family. We wait for them to come back each year." A Hong Kong businessman continues in that vein to Rosenfeld: "It's the human touch. That's what Aman has perfected. That's what keeps me coming back."[16]

The resort chain, which now includes eighteen properties throughout the world, specializes in thoughtful details designed to make people feel at ease. One former manager says the founder, Adrian Zecha, "really knew how to treat people. He spoiled an entire generation of travelers, and sparked the trend of understated elegance around the world." One of the keys of his philosophy: "The guest experience started from the staff experience, which meant management treating staff well and them treating each other with respect. Adrian used to say that it had to be Aman in the back of the house, too."[17] The staff experience must be spectacular: there is only a 1 percent turnover rate. Staggering.

In a way World-Class Elite brands have the easiest time of it. The passion maker's mark is created by the work of the few for the few at the very top of the pyramid. The journalists who cover the industries are as passionate about the products as the designer or buyer. The consumer does his own research, which is part of the fun of the pursuit, then decides where to enter the brand experience based on various quality, design, and cost benefits.

To me, the hardest goal is to achieve what is often called *masstige* (prestige in mass quantities), which must be produced without the passionate devotion of the artisans who make great luxury products. Infusing large numbers of employees with an entrepreneur's zealous belief in a brand and passion for its making is another huge barrier to most businesses.

From airlines and hotels that make up "the hospitality industry," a painful oxymoron most days of the week, to service personnel in car dealerships to checkout lines at Macy's, the slippery slide down the passion pyramid is a painful one when we hit that bottom rung. Very few products come to mind, but certainly Starbucks is one of them and Midwest Airlines is another. Google is probably a third.

So how do these companies do it?

Howard Schultz started with the passion himself: "My epiphany came in Italy in the early '70s. I saw people drinking coffee, all kinds of coffees, outside in the sunshine, morning, noon and night. I thought Americans would like this, too."[18]

A former colleague of mine, Jerry Noonan, who has worked as a vice president of Nabisco, Polaroid, and 1-800-Flowers, summed up the power of that kind of insight and the challenge it brings when I interviewed him: "Successful brand personality development is based on one clear consumer insight and thousands of small, right decisions."[19]

Clotaire Rapaille, author of *Seven Secrets of Marketing in a Multi-Cultural World*, told me, "Howard's eureka moment was tremendous; there's no doubt about that. But his timing was perfect, as well. Remember that the early '80s was a time when everyone wanted a safe place to socialize. The AIDS epidemic had scared us all out of bars. Starbucks grew as a safe haven."[20]

Howard Schultz counters that perspective. "People always tell me that they go to Starbucks to socialize," he told us when Faith Popcorn and I interviewed him for one of her books several years ago. "But we have security cameras in our shops and when you watch the videotapes, you see people talk only with the baristas, never with each other. It's wild. I wish they did socialize there."

Well, in the 24-7 world of today's coffee drinker, perhaps it is just Schultz's often-stated goal of providing a "third space" that accounts for Starbucks's success. Schultz recognized that, while we have to go to work and we have to go home, maybe there is a joy in having someplace else to go, a haven.

Rapaille, whose breakthrough work for Folgers was to figure out the archetype of coffee, is in an excellent position to explain this third space phenomenon. As he explained it to me, "The code for coffee is home; the way I know I'm getting what I'm looking for, the cue for coffee is aroma. Now think of the way a Starbucks smells when you walk into one. Your shoulders go down and you relax. You're home."

Jerry Noonan told me there's an additional ingredient. "You walk into a Starbucks," he says, "and it's not a coffee shop. These aren't minimum-wage employees, snapping gum, listing to music that sets your teeth on edge. They are not bored out of their minds. They are baristas. They have a profession."

Indeed, one of the early triumphs in the design of Starbucks was the decision to professionalize the staff through a variety of tactics, including serious training, fair wages, and access to healthcare benefits and stock options for even part-time workers. These steps bred not only enthusiasm and commitment, but a cultlike following of appreciative workers, the high watermark of which had to have been Michael Gill's book *How Starbucks Saved My Life*, the first-person narrative of a one-time high-flying advertising executive who, down on his luck, turns to Starbucks because of those healthcare benefits. And he is not alone. A doctor friend of mine confides that her sister—her lawyer sister—worked for Starbucks in order to have healthcare benefits while she was starting her own firm.

Where does this respect for the employee come from? According to a Harvard Business School case on the company, it is in the root stock—the DNA—of the company itself.

> In the exigencies of managing a brand new business, they could not always adhere to (a rough division of responsibilities). "Everyone did everything" in the small company (Dave) Olsen said. He sliced meats in the tiny business office while his partner made phone calls at the desk next to him. Schultz waited on customers, wiped counters, and checked the speed of service in the store. Baristas, such as Jennifer Ames-Karreman, and (Dawn) Pinaud, who managed the store, took part in many decisions. "We agonized over all kinds of questions, big and small, trying to make the coffee bar experience as fine as possible," Olsen said. "We debated, for example, whether a particular napkin was as good in quality as the coffee we were serving." The entire staff logged long hours. "We lived and breathed the company and its possibilities," Olsen said. "But it was not "workaholism" that drove the group. "It was risk, passion, investment, and opportunity all converging."[21]

It seems like it still is. It's hard to image that from 1986 to ten years later, this little band of passionistas could take that recipe of risk, passion, investment, and opportunity and create another nine hundred Starbucks throughout the country, plus be on the cusp of launching its first shop in Tokyo. Yet that is what happened, and it continues to happen at an unprecedented rate around the world today.

The formula at the beginning is the same today: hire people who care about coffee. Encourage them to communicate knowledge and enthusiasm to patrons. This is easy enough to say but incredibly difficult to execute. How do you ramp up for that kind of "can't catch our breath" growth? Schultz's philosophy was an expensive one: know where you're going and hire ahead of yourself. One example that the Harvard study points to is Schultz's decision to hire Howard Behar, a retail expert with more than twenty-five years experience. He was the one who counseled to continue their emphasis on the hiring and training of great people.

> He argued, for instance, that Starbucks was too product-focused, that the business needed to pay more attention to the people who make, serve, and buy coffee. Since baristas and other employees directly affected the quality of products and the consumer experience in stores, Behar said, they exerted tremendous influence on the company's performance. Committed, enthusiastic employees were much more likely to deliver good service and provide an appealing environment for customers than disenfranchised staff. The success of the business thus depended significantly on motivating and sustaining employees' interest in Starbucks's offerings, including its products, working environment, and culture.[22]

I love that idea. Employees should be motivated and their interest *sustained* in products, their working environment, and their corporate culture. That is truly transformation and, I suspect, that's where Starbucks gets its real authority. Behar apparently also urged a constant, credible concentration on the customer, telling baristas to "Just say yes" when listening to and granting patrons' requests. Amazing.

The locations themselves, tens and tens of thousands of them around the world, are powerful advertising for the brand. "Our locations are our advertising, our baristas carry our message," Schultz says. "We don't do conventional market research. Our customers tell us if they like a new idea. Our job is to lead. Nobody ever woke up saying, 'I wish I could have a mocha-cappuccino grande.' But now we have truck drivers and teachers and executives asking for them. We've taught the world to speak Starbucks."[23]

What else makes Starbucks such a welcoming haven? One element has to be the decision to let people linger longer. In defiance of a fast-food and faster-turnover restaurant world, Starbucks does not intimidate the customer who spent four bucks into leaving. Rather, there's an unwritten law that patrons can hang out there pretty much as long as they need to: notice the conveniently spaced electric sockets so all can recharge their laptop batteries?

A retail design colleague points out there's nothing in the shops to encourage moms with strollers to come in. It's far more of an adults-only hangout, although there's nothing that says mothers desperate for that respite can't enter either.

Beyond these attributes, there were also a couple of boundaries the brand was willing to cross. First, Starbucks did not limit the brand to only coffee drinkers; second, it did not limit the brand to only beverages; and third, it did not limit the brand to only Starbucks locations or its core competencies. The notion of going beyond the bean was obviously inspired. How many of us have not tried Frappuccino or a Starbucks

Double Shot, whether at a Starbucks or in a convenience store, courtesy of the Pepsi partnership? (In its first full year of sales, Frappuccino contributed $52 million in sales, roughly 7 percent of the company's revenues.) Many have bought music, a book, or a T-mobile connection at Starbucks. Still others purchase roasted, whole, or ground beans in a supermarket, courtesy of another partnership, this time with Kraft's Maxwell House. Starbucks Ice Cream is made in tandem with Dreyer's Grand. Last year, the company exited a confection agreement with Godiva and began one with Hershey's, which now makes and distributes a line of Starbucks chocolate to food, drug, mass, and convenience stores. The line includes chocolate-covered coffee beans—what's not to love?

Although Schultz probably correctly believes that this company "could put its name on toothpaste and it would sell," he hasn't gone to those extremes. But it was Schultz who introduced the Blue Note Blend of coffee with a jazz CD, produced with Capital Records and its Blue Note record label. Schultz told the Harvard Case Study author he was convinced that music was "a major part of both the environment and the soul of the Starbucks retail experience."

"Think about it," says Lori Daniel, founding partner and chief inspiration officer of Two-Chefs-on-a-Roll, the private label food maker. "In the early 1980s you could barely sell the stuff at a quarter a cup. If you asked anyone did they want to spend more to have a special coffee, they'd have stared at you. The big decisions were regular or decaf, brewed or instant. Today, we're routinely spending $2.50 to $4.50 a day, every day. Millions of us. He's spawned a cottage industry of small, mom and pop coffee shops *cum* book stores or pottery shops that simply wouldn't exist today if he hadn't been successful with Starbucks. And, what he's done for the cappuccino machine manufacturers is incredible: Every restaurant has to have one."[24]

We can read all the articles, case studies, and interviews, but of course there is the profoundly personal experience that gives us the "gut check." Mine came in 2001 when I went to Tokyo on business. The hotel accommodations I was staying in seemed more like the tiny, albeit efficiently organized, roomette one might use on board a train. There was no reason to linger in the room—no room to linger, either. Dazed by jet lag and the enigmatic street layout of Tokyo, I found the welcoming sign of a Starbucks just two blocks away. I knew I could find my way back to the hotel by 9 a.m. when my colleagues were coming to collect me. So off to Starbucks I went, surrounded by the cacophony of what was to me an impenetrable language. But I walked in, took in the aroma, and exhaled. I was home and sure enough one unfathomable language gave way to one that had once seemed nearly equally inscrutable: Starbuckese, the genuine Esperanto. I listened as this now nearly universal tongue was spoken: Latte! Frappuccino! Mochaccino! And even the occasional venti iced white mocha 2 percent no whip. I got my latte, sat down with my *USA Today*, and luxuriated in this slice of my global home away from home.

Now of course it's possible to lose one's way en route to a sustainable and loved passion brand. The well-documented stumbles—including bringing in so much food that the place no longer smelled like home *or* coffee—needed to be reversed and done so quickly. It appeared in late 2007 that Starbucks was losing some of its luster: too many shops opening too fast in too many places with too little training for staff. The consumer was looking elsewhere, enticed by the siren call of McDonald's and Dunkin' Donuts's more affordably priced coffees. Every level of the passion brand pyramid requires the fervent devotion of the makers, the baristas in Starbucks's case, to make the brand worth more than the sum of its parts.

Still, my money is on Schultz to bring Starbucks back up to code. The training day for baristas in early 2008 was more than a public relations stunt. Here's another personal "gut check." Although I normally order my coffee beans from Peet's, I'd run out one morning after that training day and I had people coming over for a breakfast meeting. So I dashed to my nearby Starbucks. The barista enthusiastically offered me a free cup of a coffee he'd just brewed and wanted my opinion. I'd only been in that store two or three times before. It wasn't that he recognized me as a frequent patron. No. It was just that he was proud of what he'd made and had the authority to share it. From a thousand small gestures like that one, I'm convinced that the passionate personality of brand Starbucks will return. And with it, the value of the experience will ultimately help the company weather current economic headwinds.

There are cautionary tales, though, of big brands stumbling due to employees who are passionate, yes, but the passion is one of anger, rage, and wrath. United Airlines offers one example, perfect in its horror. According to a news account on AOL.com, it seems a United pilot on a flight from Salt Lake City to Denver announced to the passengers that he was too upset to fly. We can just imagine the collective groan aboard that flight. One passenger paraphrased his announcement: "Some of you may have witnessed an incident I was involved with at the gate. I'm not going to go into the details, but it was an interpersonal confrontation that upset me significantly to the point where I'm not focused enough to fly you to Denver. I feel like I may not be calmed and focused enough to fly to Denver for another hour." So good for him for not flying when he felt he could put his passengers at risk. But was this a call from an ex-wife or a furious friend? Was his child upset with him? Nope. The cause of his distress was that other United crewmembers had seen him wearing his hat and were angry about that! (The United pilot's union had asked pilots to take off their hats as a solidarity signal showing their objection to the airline's decision to set aside stock worth about $130 million to fund a new executive incentive plan, while the company continued to cut routes and lay off employees.) The crewmembers' passionate fury with him for violating the union's protest so discombobulated the pilot that he could no longer fly.[25]

Not every brand, not even every passion brand, can have its own army of baristas to embody and articulate the news of the brand. Even passion brands need advertising agencies, public relations firms, promotion companies, and Web designers. The trick is to find people who are as passionate about their craft as you are about yours. Are they obsessed with the nuances of branding and building product enthusiasm as you are about the benefits and features of your product?

Specialized Bicycle Components for many years had Goodby, Berlin & Silverstein as its agency, which has since gone on to have several different iterations as the partners split apart. The GBS people were convicted both about Specialized and about GBS's ability to "get it." They developed a tone of the advertising that spoke directly to bikers. It was described as "attitudinal and edgy," but it captured the way bikers thought and talked, as well as what they said. There's a "you know it when you see it" rule that applies to passion brand marketing. It stops feeling like marketing and becomes more like the overheard internal conversation of someone thinking about buying the product. Like eavesdropping on the psyche of someone with your priorities, attitudes, and worldview. It's hard to get right, easy to get wrong, and thrilling to create a voice for the product that is as persuasive as it is honest.

One agency that has figured out the costs as well as rewards of working on passion brands is Amazon Advertising, a twelve-year-old group that boasts Kashi foods among its clients. As

Millie Olson writes in *Ad Age*, "As a young copy writer I had to muster enthusiasm for Artificially Flavored Blueberry Muffin Mix with Real Wild Maine Blueberries Inside, Cheese Slices with More Real Cheese (huh?) and Minute Gourmet, a medley of ingredients that came in a bag resembling the one you find in your airline seat pocket. I learned to focus my passion on making good ads. That's all changed. I blame it on Kashi, whose agency we've been for five years now."

According to Olson, the folks at Kashi (owned by Kellogg since 2000) "walk the talk." When the agency coined the tagline, it was "seven whole grains on a mission." Suddenly, the agency drank the client's Kool-Aid. "No more sugar-coated cereals for our families and friends," she explained. "Soon the office pantry was packed floor to ceiling with seven-whole-grain cereals, granolas, snack bars, and frozen entrées. Not only did it make our employees feel proud to work at Amazon, it helped us attract new ones. And it began to affect new business. No more lusting after big car companies (unless they're rolling out fleets of hybrids). No more sugary soft drinks, no overly processed foods." She quotes advertising legend Keith Reinhart: "A principle isn't a principle unless it costs you."

Amazon's other clients include two formidable passion brands: Peet's coffee and Mondavi wines. Olson sums up the credo: "No Super Bowl commercials here. But the joy is, you're not making anything up. It all comes straight out of the client's DNA. And, the passion comes straight from our hearts."[26]

The Martin Agency in Richmond, Virginia, seems like another group of passionate advocates of their clients' brands. The company's goal has become over the years to transform brands, not just build them. According to John Adams, agency chief executive officer, "Historically, we don't do well as incrementalists. All the clients who have shown up over the past couple of years seem to appreciate that we have a very strong sense of ambition for them."

This means that they, too, evaluate current and new business opportunities in terms of a principle, but it may also mean they have to shed some and say no to others.

Finding the right partner to tell the brand's story becomes crucial as we seek to move toward a mass brand. Midwest Airlines seems to be charting those stressful waters, although its advertising tagline, "Best Care in the Air," may not be much of a claim, given the state of air travel, these days.

The hardest task is, I believe, what Midwest Airlines seems able to deliver, which is seemingly effortlessly, day-in and day-out service in a brutish industry. It is certainly the only airline I put among my own passion brands.

The late Arthur C. Clarke said, "Any sufficiently advanced technology is indistinguishable from magic." Although air travel isn't really an advanced technology at this point, Midwest Airlines to me is magic. It uses the markers of all first-class travel—two-by-two leather seating, plus courteous, friendly, and efficient attendants—but it charges all economy rates. Simply put: I go out of my way to fly this airline. If I'm headed anywhere near the Midwest, I see if I can figure out how to fly into the airline's hub in Milwaukee. My daughter, Mattie, and I first discovered it when we started going to a family camp near Lake Elkhart in northern Wisconsin. Since then, it's become the default setting on my browser for Midwest air travel. I check there first before forcing myself to deal with other carriers. It adds some time to our drive but probably years to our lives.

As in the cases of Starbucks and American wine makers, Midwest has figured out how to have a passionate core of people who work for it. The flight attendants aren't furious, they seem to enjoy the process—they bake chocolate chip cookies on board for nearly every flight—and they are working the aisles rather than standing at the front of the plane and bickering among themselves.

Perhaps some of the passion stems from a belief, probably accurate, that if they succumb to the incipient anger on board most airplanes, they will cease having a reason for being and will be gobbled up by one of the major carriers in search of scale and efficiencies, that is, more bodies per flight, fewer perquisites per body. But I believe that a great deal of the joy one feels boarding a Midwest Airlines flight is that somehow they have managed to remember that they're going to fly today. *Fly!* They remember it's something they want to do, not have to do. They've captured some of that imaginative joy in the idea of flight. "We're flying!" And they share it with their passengers. (Of course, learning that the airline has filed for Chapter 11 protection doesn't augur well for further care in the air.)

That's what the best passion brands do for us—the very best do it through the people they choose, those who choose to show up, and indeed those who are thrilled to show up. As one passion brand worker told me, "Hell! I'd pay them to work here!"

WHAT WE TALK ABOUT WHEN WE TALK ABOUT BRANDS

Hire Passionistas

Verbatim Consumer Quotes

"I couldn't believe it. I had a problem with it and I called them. I was online for at least ten minutes before anyone came on. Then I was talking to someone in Asia someplace or India. They had no idea what my problem was or how to fix it. They just kept saying that I'd made a mistake, but they couldn't tell me how to fix it. And when I tried to take it back to the store, the guy said I had to return it to the manufacturer because it was some kind of special promotional thing. Nobody would help me. I was out two hundred dollars and the damn thing never worked."

"I walked in the store looking for a birthday present for my nephew. I have girls, so I was a little overwhelmed, but this sales lady must have seen the look in my eyes. She came right over and took me in hand. She knew the merchandise. She knew what an eight-year-old boy would like. She told me she had boys. She made it so, so easy. She wrapped it for me and I was out of there. I was so appreciative. If I could have tipped her I would have. I tell all my friends to go there now."

"I went into the bike store and they were clueless. So I took the sales guy by the hand and I made him call the manufacturer's 800-line and when he got somebody on the line, I'd ask the sales guy the question, he'd ask the guy at the company, and then he'd repeat the answer back to me. I felt like I was the parent of a naughty boy. But I made him do it; I was so angry that he'd sold me this bike and couldn't answer question number one about it."

"I remember I was looking forward to eating the chocolate, but when I got it home, it smelled funny, like it had been stored next to potpourri or something. Each piece just reeked to high heaven. I called the store but they were clueless. It was like they couldn't admit that they'd made a mistake in putting the chocolate next to the potpourri. So I called the manufacturer—it was Godiva—and they were fabulous. They sent me a big box of my favorite assortment and I didn't even have to send back the bad stuff. I never went back to that store; they sold a lot of things there, not just chocolate, but I never went back. Godiva though, that's different. They did the right thing."

"I ordered the coffee maker. It came with two carafes, I think they call them. One of them was broken. So I called KitchenAid and this fellow got on the line, he told me his name, apologized, and said to put it in the box and leave it on my front door step. The next day the old box had been picked up and a new one delivered by the time I got back from work. Just like that. It was amazing. Then, the same guy called me back two days later just to make sure it had been delivered and to make sure I liked the coffee maker and everything was okay. It really was the same guy, not just like everybody's named Tad or something. It was just so nice. You don't get that kind of follow through anymore. I was so impressed. People laughed at me and said, 'You'd better get that kind of service when you spend that much on a coffee maker,' but I didn't care. It made it seem that much more special. I don't think I've ever used the second carafe; I think it's for decaf or something, but still. It's there and it's perfect. They stood behind it."

Chapter 5

KNOW THEY KNOW YOU NEED THEM

One of the most difficult to grasp of the postmodern marketing realities is best stated by Stephen Brown, a professor at the University of Ulster and author of many fabulously well-written articles for various academic journals: "Marketers know about consumers, consumers know about marketers, marketers know consumers know about marketers, consumers know marketers know consumers know about marketers." Read it again, please: It's an Alice in Wonderland funhouse mirror that is as important to understand as it is difficult.

For Brown the insight is that today's consumers understand, nearly through osmosis if nothing else, that advertising is directed at them. They have grown up on the centrality of this attention: If they buy into a brand, it matters. They understand what the word "brand" means in pretty much the same way marketers do. They understand the power of trademarks and licensed characters literally from their first bottle: "Whatever else they are remembered for," says Brown, "they are and always will be, Generation™."[1]

BRANDING PROCESS STEP 4

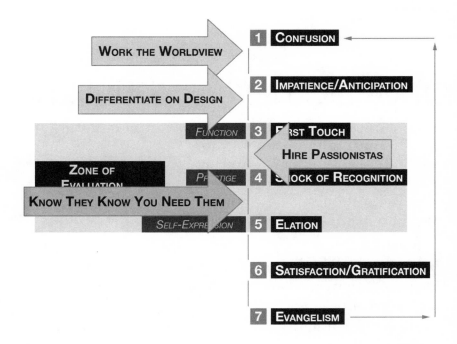

In my own work I can corroborate this vision: There are virtually no unfocused group people left in the world. The consumer is "in" the world of the marketing professional. Listen to them talk about "what the brand is trying to do here" and "if they want to get me to try this, they'd better . . ." and "I get the objective, but I don't like this strategy."

Should we need further proof, we need only tune into the incredibly popular series *Mad Men* on the AMC network. Yes, of course, Darren Stevens was in advertising on *Bewitched*. There have been some movies that have used the industry as a backdrop, but the unprecedented response to this cable channel series is really a remarkable testimony to the population's interest in the idea of marketing, and, of course, its roots in the three-martini lunch. It's one thing to have the water cooler effect for a series about some "made men" in the New Jersey suburbs, or four female friends tripping down Fifth Avenue in their Manolos or tippling Cosmopolitans at Scout's (really O'Neal's Speakeasy). It's quite another for us to be obsessed about the weekly goings-on of a bunch of sexist, racist, smoking, drinking, philandering, anti-Semitic, Bryl-creemed WASP guys from the 1960s. And yet we are.

"What do women want?" asks one.

"Who cares," replies his boss.

The series is moving beyond television, inspiring commercials, designer fashions, window displays at Bloomingdale's, merchandise, CDs, calendars—even *Ad Age* brought out a mock 1960s issue, declaring that Sterling Cooper, the fictitious agency, "Wins Kodak Projector Account."

The appeal of the show must be beyond the core of people directly involved with advertising. Or it illustrates that all of us are directly involved with advertising and we want to understand our roots.

Academics I spoke with concur: The consumer is tremendously aware of being the target of marketing. So rather than be in denial, brand strategists need to do the "heavy lifting" of figuring out how to eschew traditional tactics that interrupt a favorite show in order to deliver a monologue and to create new engagement techniques that forge a more personal and relevant dialogue. This is easier said than done, of course. Still, there is GEICO.

Think about trying to find a less-interesting category: Could there be anything more commoditized than auto insurance? Maybe, but I'm pretty sure I wouldn't want to try to identify it. Yet, here's a mass marketer in a low-interest category that's managed to forge a passion brand. It's an anomaly, really, a mass marketer selling a service directly to customers, spending big dollars in traditional media and using buzz as a multiplier effect to turbo-charge those dollars.

Essentially GEICO has pioneered the direct-to-consumer auto insurance industry. Getting there first with the clearest message was crucial. While scores of confused marketers attempted to "educate" the consumer on the value of buying auto insurance direct, GEICO realized that all people needed to hear was "15 minutes can save you 15 percent on auto insurance." Boom. That's it.

Having staked out the simple, easy-savings message, GEICO's competitors were forced to get in line, each taking a more complicated or niche position. The economy of messaging left GEICO poised to evolve various ways to bring interest to their message—making a virtue of the repetition and building a substantial network for GEICO content. The playfulness of intertwining GEICO and the gecko started the process.

The campaign——all the brain child or, better said, children —of the Martin Agency in Richmond, Virginia, began, legend has it, on a bar napkin, as the brand and the agency tried to figure out how to get people to pronounce the company's name correctly. The gecko's first appearance was meant to be his last, as well; just a simple fifteen-second spot to get the name thing handled. Then there was the Screen Actors Guild strike in 1999. The crew had to make do without high-priced talent. The gecko made a comeback.

The personality of that charming—is he an Aussie for some reason?—gecko began the endearing of the brand to the viewer. For the next couple of years, he was the star of the show: auditioning first to become the "spokescritter," becoming the GEICO Employee of the Month, then finding true love.

The concern became one that many celebrities face: over-exposure. Since the brand appeals to a broad range of drivers, from first-timer teens to yoga moms to boomers and folks driving slowly around a gated retirement community, there was worry that enough was more than too much.

Reportedly, the folks at the Martin Agency then unleashed multiple creative teams to figure out new approaches. In 2003 they launched the "Good News" campaign. Remember? The description of a horrible misfortune followed by the good news that "I just saved a lot of money on my car insurance."

Then came the caveman series, running simultaneously with the gecko ads, but pointing out in an entirely different way that the GEICO concept is so simple, "even a caveman . . ." (and spawning a not so good but very brief TV series, which is wild, when you think of it). The idea was to land a bunch of meterosexual cavemen who had somehow survived for millennia but were incensed about the GEICO slogan. It became so popular that the company launched a Web site, Cavemanscrib.com, taking us behind the scenes to their twenty-first century lair.

Next came a series of pairings of real customers with spokespeople cum voiceover artists to narrate their stories: Little Richard, Burt Bacharach, and Peter Graves all appeared to help translate various tales of woe.

The Martin Agency's Mike Hughes, executive creative director, explained to the entrepreneurial business magazine *Fast Company* that, as he saw the various campaigns play out simultaneously, he realized they'd created a better way to brand. "Once upon a time," said Hughes, "an ad was about a company's unique selling position. But people can now accept more complex brands and I thought we might be able to build a deeper relationship if we built on multiple fronts."

It is a fascinating triptych of advertising really, selling us but beyond that entertaining us with a wink in the direction of commerce. We know we're being marketed to, but we're appreciative of the wit and acknowledgment that it doesn't have to be a painful process. GEICO gets us.

But does it work? Beyond the fact that these charming ads keep evolving, I have a more personal response. After years of living in the city without a car, I finally succumbed and bought one a few months ago. As I was arranging the pick-up with the salesman, he reminded me that I needed to have auto insurance in place on the day I came to drive it away. The conversation went something like this:

HIM: "So you'll need to have insurance cards."
ME: "Yes, you're right."
HIM: "Do you have an agent or a policy or will you just call GEICO?"
ME: "I'll go online to GEICO."
HIM: "Terrific. They're fast."

And so they were. My salesman gave me the vehicle identification number and I went online to geico.com. Within two minutes I was printing out the insurance cards. This is no exaggeration. It was simple, fast, and I assume fairly priced, although I absolutely did not shop around. The brand's personality had engaged me and made me aware of it, pushing out other brands or alternatives like finding an agent, with panache.

This personality trumped the claims of other longtime entrants like All State or State Farm for me, even other online brands like Progressive, although I make the assumption that pretty much each of these would have fair pricing and simple procedures. As Stephen Brown points out, "We live in a world where all products, services, brands, experiences—whatever— are pretty much functionally equivalent and there is very little to choose among them in terms of performance."[2]

And yet choose we must. I don't want or need four auto insurance policies. So the play is to personality, wit, and engagement with the marketing. "Today's consumers," Brown writes, "are wise to the wiles of marketers. They possess a 'marketing reflex,' an inbuilt early warning that detects incoming commercial messages and automatically deletes them."[3]

Said a different way, Jonathan Bond and Richard Kirshenbaum of the Kirshenbaum & Bond agency write in their book *Under the Radar—Talking to Today's Cynical Consumer*: "Consumers are like roaches. We spray them with marketing and for a time it works. Then inevitably they develop an immunity, a resistance."[4] Perhaps what GEICO has figured out is how to forestall the development of that immunity. Perhaps three campaigns are really better than one, keeping us intrigued not just with the content of each but with the fact of three. What is going on here? What are they up to now?

"People are so aware they are being marketed to," one professor tells me. "Brands that understand their audience on a personal level and seem to reject traditional marketing techniques in favor of more personal approaches are the ones that 'get it.'" One of the significant benefits of "getting it" is forging a dialogue with the consumer that goes beyond a commercial codependency and develops into a genuine relationship.

Perhaps what GEICO has been able to do is what marketing theorists are just getting wise to. The prevailing winds of academia were once positive that consumers divided their opinions of brand by a schism between a functional or symbolic brand, with symbolic nearly always meaning prestigious. Theories of brand concept management said that only one road could be trod. The brand had to be demonstrably better in some meaningful way ("richer taste!" "Corinthian Leather," "twice as much and only a nickel too") or it must stand for something meaningful (if you drive this car, it means you're <u>fill in the blank</u>).

However, consumers now seem to be revealing themselves to be more able to handle complexity in their brands. Prestige is not the only reason for choosing a symbolic brand; self-expression is a rising reason. Consumers want their brands to "express my personality" and to be "elegant," "exciting" "distinctive." There may indeed be a continuum. First, functional goals must be met, then symbolic goals can be attached to make these powerful associations with consumers.[5]

We may start with a Timex or Casio but work our way up to a Movado, Cartier, Omega, Rolex, even an Audemars Piguet or a Piaget. The meaning of function moves from an internal question, as in "Does it tell the correct time?" to an external one, as in "What else does it say about me?"

Thus, a Volkswagen is a symbolic brand, which functions well and reliably—*and* allows its owner to make a personal statement through its branding. But it is not a mark of prestige. In a time when all products work pretty well, the symbolic benefits become increasingly important. The parentage of the brand, too, increases in importance: Who made it? What is their environmental policy? What are their labor practices?

Essentially, consumers are now on to the power of symbolism and are taking a very personal approach to which brands best express their worldviews. The endgame is that we're each becoming our own brands and using the symbols of various products to support the marketing of ourselves, whether it is as we walk down the street listening to an iPod or a Zune, decide on being a Facebook or a MySpace user, or wear True Religion or Gap jeans.

One of the places where the codependency between consumer and product can become riotously clear is in the development of sports team loyalty. Fans know that owners and players need them in a very straightforward way. No fans, no team.

The ways in which sports brands evolve a passionate following can be a great model for rethinking other brand relationships. In sports the single-minded focus is on fan identification. One model put forward by William Sutton and colleagues from the University of Massachusetts in *Sports Marketing Quarterly* looks like this:

SUTTON/SPORTS MARKETING QUARTERLY GRAPH

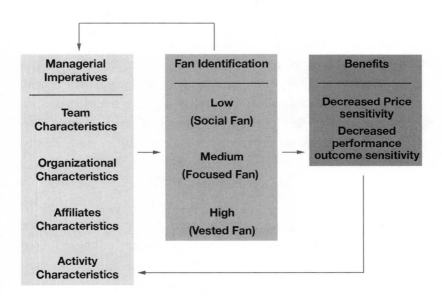

One of the outcomes of a great sports franchise—the Boston Red Sox is one example, with its long dry spell between World Series trophies—is to "decrease performance outcome sensitivity," as this model puts it, but we might otherwise think of this as loving the team whether it wins or loses. I can't help but believe that what we see with these successful sports franchises must be more than a bit applicable to the world of brands, particularly in how forgiving we are if a treasured brand stumbles.

However, we don't start with that goal in mind. Rather, the idea is that successful teams and seasons tend to help fans move from low involvement to medium, or medium to high.

There is a bandwagon effect that success brings. Another element that success brings: the desire of fans to brand themselves with team paraphernalia, which of course increases multiple revenue streams.

This becomes incredibly important as we consider some of the demographic trends that are moving consumers inexorably toward isolation. "Although people in the US society are becoming disconnected from a sense of community as a result of changing lifestyles, societal interests and technological innovations, interestingly this does not hold true for spectator sports," Sutton writes. "Spectator sports are deeply rooted in place—meaning a key expression of community identification and expression. Sport promotes communication, involves people jointly, and provides common symbols, a collective identity and a reason for solidarity."[6]

"Our (LA Lakers') collective success has forged some kind of unity in this huge and fragmented metropolis and it cuts across class cultural lines," said retired basketball star Kareem Abdul-Jabbar.[7]

The second managerial trait that affects fans is the organization itself. This is the off-the-field performance of the ownership and the players, as well as an understanding of the tradition of the franchise and reputation. Does the ownership have a commitment to the community, to excellence—as evidenced by investment in facilities, managers, and players—and to integrity in every level of team business? Do the team members behave well off the field or court? How does their behavior reflect on the team and how does it seem to personally reflect on the fan?

The "affiliate characteristics" is really an academic term for BIRG—basking in reflective glory. A study done in 1976 of college students found that students used "we" to describe how their team did when it won and "they" when it lost. Thus, here we have the individual's need to belong, which can be met by a sports team through association with the larger community of fans all sharing the same joys and failures. This bonding can bring even strangers together, as in season ticket holders seated next to one another who become such good friends throughout the season that they create a social connection that outlives the year's race.

Finally, activity characteristics are the ways in which we can participate as fans with our team: certainly at the ballpark, but also—as my brother and father did for so many summers in my childhood—listening to the game on the radio; watching it via Dish, cable, or broadcast television; keeping tabs on the score over the Internet; and even IMing friends about key plays. One great thing most teams have going for them now is the Internet. The Web sites of sports teams are among the most exciting and connecting for fans.

The San Francisco 49ers football team and the Boston Red Sox baseball franchises both seem to have been able to move their fans' identification from the low (social) to the medium (focused) and up to the high (vested) level, and to have done it on a national level rather than on a purely geographic basis. The results of our omnibus survey showed the widespread appeal of these two teams. This can, it seems, be explained in good part by the management imperatives reported on in the model, but also, I suspect, by some marketing efforts done right by the franchises with the specific goal of increasing fan identification with the teams.

Among these tactics are increased player and team accessibility to the public (these guys aren't just around for the games but also live in the area and show up in local restaurants); a high level of local community involvement with activities and charities, philanthropies, and other neighborhood outreach initiatives; strong emphasis on pride in the team's history and tradition; and the enabling and encouragement of fan clubs are all ways in which teams routinely work to deepen the fans' identification in the sport.

These teams' Web sites are chock-full of ways for fans to become involved with the team. Ways that go well beyond passive watching. National anthem singing auditions; "your name here" 49er jerseys; brand-new Red Sox commemorative photos and coins; 49ersfaithful.net, where fans meet fans; a ring raffle so that Red Sox fans can have a chance to win a World Series ring or a C30 Volvo with the proceeds benefiting the Red Sox Foundation; the Pasta Bowl, to which fans are invited to enjoy dinner with the 49ers; a video replay corner for great plays from recent Red Sox games; an Ask-a-49er-Player section of the Web site; a Red Sox charity auction for dugout seats; 49er mobile alerts. The fan-involving activities go on and on.

It's curious why other brands don't use these mechanisms as well. Some of these fan reinforcers are transportable: One study shows that people who go on a consumer product company's factory tour are much more likely to stay loyal to the brand and recommend it to others. What other "fan" activities could be applied freshly to other products for which consumers already have a budding affection? Is this too much pressure to put on a brand?

Consider what historian Daniel Boorstin had to say about this brand community concept in 1974: "The modern American, then, was tied, if only by the thinnest of threads and by the most volatile, switchable loyalties, to thousands of other Americans in nearly everything he ate or drank or drove or read or used. Old-fashioned political and religious communities now became only two among many new, once unimagined fellowships. Americans were increasingly held to others not by a few iron bonds, but by countless gossamer webs knitting together their lives."[8] Brand webs, gossamer and otherwise, are proving to be pretty strong intermediaries.

One car company that has figured this out pretty well seems to be Jeep, which sponsors Camp Jeep (a national rally with off-road driving opportunities), Jeep Jamboree (regional rallies with a focus on off-road trail driving), and Jeep 101 (a touring off-road driving course). Taken together, these events are thought of as brandfests and academically defined as "a specialized, non-geographically bound community, based on a structured set of social relationships among users of a brand."[9]

The researchers, reporting in the *Journal of Marketing*, worked to conduct ethnographies on site at these events, as well as to analyze data from a quantitative perspective. Ethnographies are marketing research tools borrowed from the world of anthropology; they require researchers to observe consumers as they are "in the wild," that is, in this case, as they go off-roading and mix with members of the brand and each other.

The researchers found tremendous sales and marketing effects resulting from this kind of brand immersion, both for novice and veteran Jeep owners. One significant finding was that impassioned owners bred other owners, many times converting family members or other people within their social circle to Jeeps. Note this description from a couple (Cherokee owners) who attended one event:

Woman: "A number of people have bought 'em (Jeep Cherokees) since we've bought."

Man: "Yeah, it's sort of like it's just grown in to a circle of people. The people that we initially—before children—we used to hang out a lot with, three or four of them have Jeeps of some kind or . . ."

Woman: "They all lived in this little cul-de-sac, and they all owned Jeep Cherokees! I mean you didn't move there unless you (laughing) had a Cherokee!"

Another participant described a three-year series of Jeep sales, beginning with his own and ending with three siblings and his father buying Jeeps.

At the Jeep events, drivers were taught—in some cases by Jeep instructors and in others by veteran Jeep owners—many tips on how to use their vehicles ethically and responsibly off-road. For many it seems to have been an opportunity to learn how to use the many features on their vehicles that had gone untried. For others it was the chance to demonstrate mastery. But for all it was a bonding opportunity with their cars, to the Jeep brand, to the Jeep/Chrysler company, and to each other.

Here's another interview excerpt. Woman: "I love my Jeep now. I liked it before, but now I feel like we're a team."

One fellow who owned an Explorer—he'd been brought to the event by a friend—expressed disappointment in his own vehicle and now aspired to owning a Jeep. "I just had the most amazing time. My dad's friend is the dealership guy, you know, the Ford guy? So I don't want to mock him or anything, but (the Wrangler) kills my Explorer. My Explorer's a Limited. It has air suspension, all this special crap. And it just destroys my Explorer."

When asked if he'd feel comfortable doing the course with his Explorer, he says, "I don't think so. I think it might tip, actually." Reportedly, he left wanting to buy a new Jeep, a phenomenon that the researchers saw repeated several times over.

One woman, a recent convert, was thrilled to have someone drive with her when she was learning to negotiate off-road terrain. Another enjoyed the attention of several other owners who taught her how to take the doors off for a more open experience. Most were impressed that Jeep would go to the trouble of sponsoring the events. Many expressed that a feeling of "family" had emerged.

Basically, the researchers found that it was this element of interpersonal connection, however temporary, at the Jeep events that moved the needle. Current neophyte Jeep owners were made happier with their purchase because of an expanded understanding of its various functions and utilities. Seasoned owners were made less happy with their current models once they'd tried out the most recent edition, thereby heightening and hastening plans to get a new Jeep. Everyone felt a sense of brand belonging, not stranded alone with a car but rather engaged and part of something infinitely larger and much more fun, with a proud heritage each hoped to extend. These events seem to accrue benefits to Jeep along many dimensions. The model looks like this:

FOCAL CUSTOMER GRAPH

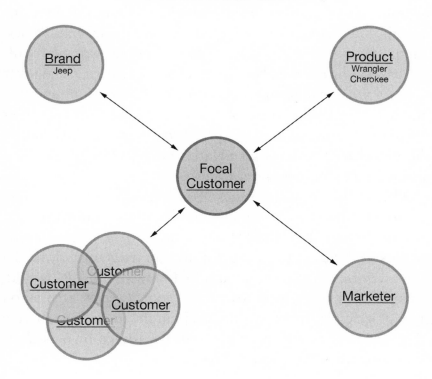

An important element the model highlights is the role of marketers who are at the events. This isn't something to off-load to an event-planning firm and check a Blackberry for attendance figures in the late afternoon. No. If these marketers want their consumers to be engaged in the brand, they must be there, too.

One of the participants interviewed at a Jeep 101 meeting called his fifteen-year-old son over and introduced him as "the next generation of Wrangler owner." The son ardently agreed. This sense of brand lineage on the consumer side of the equation is often overlooked, most probably because bonuses don't take into account the lifetime value of consumers and their families for generations to come.

Car buyers and owners seem particularly passionate and eager to participate in brand communities. The Porsche Club of America is another private world constructed with the owners and enthusiasts in mind. It offers multiple rallies, annual events, and monthly dinners. One participant recalls the passion of the members hotly debating whether it's better to wash a Porsche from the top down or the bottom up. Two hundred thousand owners of the Volkswagen Golf GTI meet annually in an Austrian lake site setting to extol the virtues of this model for four days. The Harley Owners Group (HOG) is also legendary among motorcyclists.

One of the unifying themes of such groups is that they are proud of what they are and what they own, and they are proud of what they *are not* and would never own. Porsche owners feel themselves superior to Corvette owners in the same way that Apple enthusiasts look down on the PC world. This sense of opposition to the big brands seems a common thread. It's easier to be passionate about the underdog than the "big guy," so it's not surprising that no Toyota owners clubs have surfaced.

Consumers need and want to experience their brands in new and emerging ways, and brands need consumers in the same old way—sales. But the same old ways to achieve brand awareness, trial, purchase, and loyalty eventually stop working and we're required to approach the relationship anew. It's not enough to get consumers to buy the brand; we have to help them help us market it to their peers, their social network, and their families. They know it, and we ignore it our own peril.

WHAT WE TALK ABOUT WHEN WE TALK ABOUT BRANDS

Know They Know You Need Them

Verbatim Consumer Quotes

"I knew it was some kind of script, right? Like he was reading a bunch of questions somebody else had made up and he didn't care one way or the other about, so I started messing with him. I'd answer in French or Spanish or Pig Latin. That got his attention! I'd mean, I'd call in to make a complaint—which he wasn't able to help me with, oh by the way—and here he is reading off some laundry list of 'Have I answered your question with excellence?' and 'How else may I share our commitment to satisfied customers?' kind of scripted BS, I just wanted him to come to. I felt like slapping him, Hey! This isn't how you get my business. You need me, jerk!"

"You walk in and it's like the night of the living dead in there. I mean, I know they work on a commission, but you'd think it didn't matter in the slightest. They're talking to each other, checking their cell phones, doing anything to avoid making eye contact or heaven forbid, trying to help me. I say they deserve what's going to happen to them. They'll be out of business in a year, I know it."

"So, I'd read all about Lexus service and everything, but I still didn't want to have to deal with a car salesman. I just went online and plugged in what I was looking for in a used car. I'd have thought that I'd have heard from someone pretty quickly. It took a month before anybody at Lexus even acknowledged my call. And then it was just because some computer program somewhere generated an e-mail to me about "How do you rank our service?" So I let fly. I answered the e-mail with all the details of how I'd tried to get in touch with them to buy a car and nobody could be bothered. I bet I ruined somebody's bonus. They get ranked on stuff like that and I hope it hurt."

"I know that the comment cards mean something to their sales people, so I took the time to fill it out. I mean she'd really, really helped me in a jam. She got the alterations done that day, so I wanted to do what I could to help her. I'd heard that if they get so many positive comments or compliments or whatever it means a promotion or some kind of bonus, and I wanted to do my part."

"It just seemed cheesy. I mean here's this supposedly terrific product and it's kind of what? Like dancing all around kind of trying to get me to notice it. It felt desperate. I mean it's good or it's not, right? You don't need to be so eager to please. Hey! Look at me! Do you like me now? How about now? I'd be embarrassed to use a brand like that—my friends would think I was creepy too, or that I liked that kind of thing. Just be, you know. Just be. I'll like you or I won't, but be who you are, even if you're a brand. Don't be who you think I think you ought to be. Frantic. Desperate. Makes me anxious just thinking about it, sitting here."

Chapter 6
DEMOCRATIZE THE BRAND

Brand democracy is undoubtedly the hardest of the accelerators to deliver on, at least today. The promise is powerful: To have such a close identification between the brand and its consumers that the brand channels their hopes, desires, and needs. It responds to those *wishes*, quickly and well. Indeed, the distinction between consumer and brand maker blurs, or better, a continuum emerges, made up of individuals involved to greater or lesser degrees with the destiny of the brand.

There seem to be four styles of brand democratization, going from easiest to a bit harder to extremely difficult. The first is the *status quo*: Brands develop product and marketing ideas and take them to consumers for evaluation via focus groups, online panels, or, in some cases, test marketing. This acknowledgment of the ultimate primacy of the consumer's perspective is generations old, and most of us have participated in it in some way or other. Products and marketing ideas do become refined in these settings, rounding the hard edges of

BRANDING PROCESS STEP 5

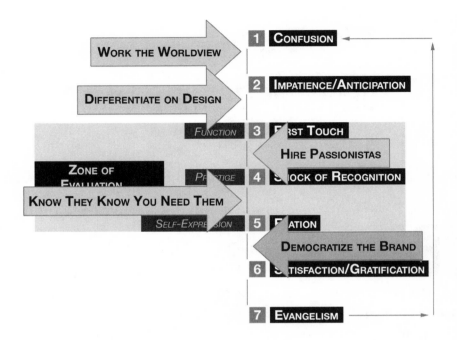

a concept to meet the sometimes amorphous consumer desire and ensuring that the benefits are communicated in a way the consumer understands.

The next level can be loosely described as *coproduction*, as in pumping my own gas, doing most of my banking at an ATM, perhaps designing and then buying my auto insurance online.

Then there's *comarketing*, which engages the consumer to help develop marketing materials, such as—in early eras—creating jingles and slogans, and evolving into consumer-generated Web content, commercials, and promotions.

Finally, there's the real deal—*coownership*. This is a level of brand engagement that partners consumer and manufacturer as equal stewards of the brand's evolution.

I think of these as the circles on a bull's-eye target, starting from the outermost ring and moving inward to that ultimate goal, in which the consumer is as passionate about the brand as its maker and the maker is as passionate as the consumer.

THE OUTERMOST RING: THE STATUS QUO

In my experience, here's how it goes. Someone in a section of a company called something like Consumer Insights has an idea, or maybe it's someone in product development or in brand management. But it starts with an idea. Then, someone like me gets called in to go see if consumers have the same idea, or like the idea, or have a better idea.

Case in point: Nabisco's new products guru Kathy Parker called me in early 2002 to say that she thought there was some "white space," which is corporate speak for unmet consumer need around the world of the in-store bakery. The company had noticed that while once the grocery store bakeries had been something very special, they had deteriorated. They were no longer the place where the consumer looked first for fresh-baked goods because it was obvious the products were being shipped to the stores from a central bakery; the areas in which the products were sold were being sprayed with a "fresh-baked" scent that came straight from an aerosol can.

Working with Hal Goldberg, we hypnotized scores of men and women around the country to get at their first, most powerful and most recent experiences with in-store bakeries, as well as with other baked goods products. Sure enough, the consumers were wise to the wiles of the stores, relying on their wares only for emergencies, as when it was time to bring St. Patrick's Day cupcakes to a Brownie Scout meeting, or for an "emergency" birthday party. What also emerged was that there were many, many acceptable alternatives. The drivers seemed to be twofold: (1) Was this a treat for every day or a special occasion? (2) Was this a treat for kids or adults?

Nearly all the available substitutes fit neatly in this needs state model. This graphic is designed to identify the kinds of brands that are best suited to various consumers' needs at various moments in time. My need this morning to take a treat to Mattie's third-grade classroom to celebrate her birthday can be easily solved by a bakery in a grocery store. But for the party tomorrow night for adults and kids, something else indeed is required, something that requires a drive across town to a very special bakery and the pothole-obsessed drive home is a special mission, indeed.

The matrix we developed looked like this.

ADULT/EVERYDAY/SPECIAL/KIDS MATRIX

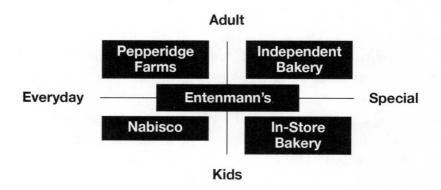

With the in-store bakery filling only this limited need for special-occasion baked goods products for kids, and with Nabisco brands' strong relationship with kids, it was so far, so good. We kept probing to find what would constitute the essentials of a bakery: cakes, pies, doughnuts, cookies, brownies, pastries, and bagels. This was a bit more difficult. Obviously we could figure out cookies and maybe even cakes and brownies, but the rest started to seem daunting. Could there be a strategic alliance or acquisition that could get us the rest of the way?

We continued to explore, but consumers started pushing us in a different direction. Their memories under hypnosis began to coalesce into the archetype for sweet baked goods products: mother's love. And the way we know our mother loves us is that the cookie melts in our mouth. With men, it was a very simple system: "My mother baked my favorite cake for my birthday. I took one bite and it just melted in my mouth. I could feel and taste her love." What did you do? "I told her I loved her."

With women, it was a bit more complex: "My mother baked my favorite cake for my birthday. I took one bite and it just melted in my mouth. I knew she loved me. But, if she loved me so much, why did she addict me to something that put fat on my thighs?"

Both men and women were aware of calories, carbs, and the siren call of a cookie package at 3 a.m. The women were particularly articulate about not wanting to "addict" their own daughters. So, in many cases, they were trying to avoid the cookie aisle. They reasoned that if they didn't bring it into the house, they could avoid the whole problem. Of course this doesn't really work. There's a moment when we succumb to the joy of a sweet baked goods treat, whether for ourselves or because we know our child, or husband, or guests coming for dinner will enjoy it.

The idea for Nabisco that began to emerge was the need to create a safety valve, a way for women specifically, since they are the primary grocery store shoppers, to feel safe to venture down the cookie aisle. The project turned from creating an alternative to an in-store bakery to the creation of a "fail safe" brand that would give women the joy of a cookie treat without the dark side of overindulgence.

We still thought that perhaps a strategic alliance with a company like Weight Watchers might work. Or perhaps we could resuscitate the SnackWell's appeal with such a product. Here's where a great company takes a great concept and makes it their own. I lobbied hard for a SnackWell's reinvigoration. But Nabisco, working with its product development people, thought the opportunity presented itself to create a new sub-brand to straightforwardly declare the product benefit across most of their lines of cookie products: the 100 Calorie Pack. The rest, as they say, is history. They launched it, and within the first couple of years it grew to a $1 billion franchise, setting the standard for the rest of the industry, which quickly followed suit with other hundred-calorie entrants. It was definitely in that moment a passion brand, breeding via the word of mouth of thrilled consumers.

Consumers had a tremendous role in this process. They literally curved the trajectory of the project from its original genesis point, namely, the in-store bakery, to create a product that responds flawlessly to valid needs. This is how the consumer products business works when it works best. Nothing happens without an idea, but the idea must be allowed to grow, morph, and shape shift until it fits the consumers' as-yet-unarticulated wish.

However, the creation of a genuine brand democracy must go beyond the "democracy" of the market, though we do "vote" by buying the brands we think are worth our money.

This is the world I spend time in, lurking behind the one-way mirror of focus group facilities and tracking consumers as they shop to create anthropologically valid ethnographies. This understanding of the consumers' unarticulated needs is necessary but not sufficient to really forge a brand democracy.

As Procter & Gamble has put it for generations, these well-managed firms seek "to build superior products that respond to consumer needs and market them supremely well." So surely that is part of the construction of great brands, some of which, like Tide-to-Go, Febreze, and Swiffer, rise to the level of passion among their many users.

But brand stewards must go beyond classic research methodology to really create a brand democracy. And the default setting isn't simply having a Web presence. It's creating Web engagement that matters. Indeed, Web-based consumer research companies abound, offering tools to engage the consumer for brand advancement.

Communispace.com offers to create "private online communities" to enable marketers to "engage and listen to your customers," citing strategy and product innovations for Hallmark's Shoebox cards, Unilever's AXE, that teen boy body spray that has become the bane of many mothers' existences, and Kraft's South Beach Diet products as examples of the process in action. CoyneBehamShouse, a favorite of mine, run by Doug Shouse, offers an equivalent service, specializing in "engagement marketing." Among the reasons they offer for engaging the consumer:

- Creating relationships that connect consumers to your brand by connecting them to each other in strong, brand-reinforcing communities
- Encouraging active participation in your brand through consumer-generated content
- Leveraging the power of your brand's core passionate enthusiast

Even all of these are fine and good, as far as they go in their efforts to enhance a company's marketing efforts. When I asked Stephen Brown, that really smart guy at the University of Ulster who proffered up that amazing funhouse mirror quote about postmodern marketing, why brands don't do more to engage consumers beyond conventional research tactics, his answer was as immediate as it was clear: "I blame marketing research and the marketing concept more generally. Conventional market research and marketers' preoccupation with customer centricity give rise to bland brands.

"People think in terms of what they know and studying what they know perpetuates this process. Many passion brands, I suspect, were not developed by focus group and so forth (Apple springs to mind here). Managers are constrained by conventional marketing wisdom and a safety-first mind-set. I suspect most managers *are* aware of passion brands and would dearly love a passion brand of their own, but they won't get there with the aid of passionless market and consumer research."[1]

Here he's articulating cogently why I've found hypnosis to be such a terrific research technique. But it's hard to get major companies to agree to it, scared as they are of showing up on the front page of the *New York Times* as having hypnotized consumers to purchase their wares. But it is through the use of such tactics that once we've broken out of the "safety first" mode allows us to understand what it is consumers are really looking for from their brand choices.

THE SECOND RING: COPRODUCTION

Sometimes it's called disintermediation, as in getting rid of the people in between the customer and the transaction. Certainly it provides for a level of customization that allows me to have precisely what I want at a cost of time and money—and a reduction of financial and social risk—that makes coproduction advantageous to both me and the brand.

Perhaps the earliest manifestation was the supermarket, the movement from the clerk assembling items from my list to me shopping the aisles, loading the cart, bringing it to the check-out line, and bagging the lot. Certainly, my own delight in Fresh Direct is a twenty-first-century example of grocery shopping as an engaging coproduction. Another fabulous example of customization is Starbucks, which—through all its permutations of beans, sizes, milks, and choices among regular, espresso, latte, Frappuccino, Mochaccino, and on and on—offers eighty-seven thousand different ways to get our coffee the way we want it, precisely. All we need do is learn the language, tell it to the barista, pay, listen as it is shouted out, wait, move to another station to retrieve it, go to yet another station, add our desired levels of desired sweetener, and, at last, sit down or race outside and enjoy.

Another emerging coproduction brand is IKEA Furniture, with its essential accessibility of the design, price, and wit— but with a postproduction creativity that engages people in a way that goes well beyond the business model. We're not talking here about the straightforward do-it-yourself aspect of IKEA's offering, the "follow our directions and you'll have a bed" business, although that surely is coproduction. But beyond that there's an emerging collective called IKEA Hackers, which views IKEA products not as finished goods, but as works in progress.

The founder of ikeahacker.blogspot.com, Mei Mei Yap, who lives in Kuala Lumpur, Malaysia, coordinates the online world of people who love to take the raw IKEA material and modify it to their personal uses; people like Winnie Lam, who made her Chocolate Sundae Toppings footstool with bags of cotton pom-poms hot-glued to an IKEA stool. Or the folks who took a seven-hundred-dollar IKEA desk lamp and retro-fitted it to become a wall sconce. Or the ones who used a stain-less steel shelving to craft a coffee table.

"I think IKEA just makes it easy to do-it-yourself because it already has a system in place of mixing and matching this frame with that cabinet and those knobs," Yap explained to a reporter for the *New York Times*. "Hacking just takes it a little further, repurposing it to fit your needs. And maybe the geek-nerd in us hackers feels a buzz having outsmarted the IKEA system by creating something of our own."[2]

A trend spotter at J. Walter Thompson, an established, world-renowned ad firm, told the *Times* in the same article, "Customization is so huge for a demographic that's skewing younger and younger. They don't want to be told by 'the man' what they should consume and how exactly they should con-sume it. That's boring. They can make their own playlist. They can take a product and make it truly their own."

This style of über-coproduction is sometimes called "cor-ruption," as consumers work to make the product uniquely their own. The classic example of corruption is the way guys buy jeans way too big and keep them perched precariously on their hips in order to mimic the way prisoners wear uniforms that don't fit and then continue to wear their pants once released as proof of "hard-time cred."

Of course, pretty quickly the brand can take the leadership of the brand back, as when major clothing manufacturers start cutting their jeans to mirror prison chic. An example of this, straight from the IKEA crate, is Deutsch Advertising hiring Brooklyn artist John Hobbs to create familiar New York scenes entirely out of IKEA's famed flat pack boxes. There was a ninety-six-foot-long, sixteen-foot-high replica of the Brooklyn Bridge, another of the Empire State Building, and one of the water-tower rooftop scenes familiar to anyone with something of a view. This project was undertaken to help celebrate the opening of the Brooklyn Red Hook IKEA, which is a story in itself: every big-box retailer from WalMart on down has tried to open a store somewhere within New York City, and each and every one has been fought off, except IKEA, which perhaps through all of its brand accessibility has emerged not as "they" but as part of "we."

The essential excitement here is to extend our horizons beyond the consumer's purchase of our goods all the way through the entire process of consumption. One writer suggests that today's consumer is not unlike the natives of South America under the colonizing Spanish. They didn't so much defy Christian missionaries as developed or appropriated the symbols of Christianity in service to their own culture. So consumers today use and convert the received world of goods to their own unique purpose.

According to the academics who study such things, there are five enablers to the coproduction process where brands and the people who use them cross paths. The first is the *background situation*: There have to be the right cultural, economic, and technologic preconditions. So we rule out emerging and growth markets, such as third world countries, and focus on mature markets with high per capita incomes, such as the United States and the European common market countries, for example.

Second, there needs to be the *correct calculus of price, time, and performance benefits, mixed with performance and social risk reduction.* What does relying on one brand require of me in terms of my money and money, two finite commodities. Next I perform the evaluation process, indexing that expenditure of resources to how efficiently the brand delivers against my needs and expectations. Then there is the requirement for an emotional component, that is, how personally important are those needs and expectations before I am willing to spend social currency to recommend the brand.

I may want to buy my airline tickets on Orbitz for any of a number of reasons. It's wildly convenient: I can book at 2 p.m. or 2 a.m. There's no waiting to hear back from a travel agent. It promises the best price. As one consumer put it, "I don't need to get a better price than anyone else, I just don't want to pay more than anyone else." It allows me to book hotels, rental cars, car services, and it makes sure the miles are deposited in my loyalty program accounts. Its computer also calls my cell phone to confirm my flight and to let me know if there are changes or delays. It even offers to let me share my airport or airline information directly with other travelers, which is a classic example of coproduction.

All this is good and just and honest. But what makes me passionate about Orbitz is that one day when a Friday afternoon flight was cancelled and it looked like I couldn't get home, someone there noticed (or some*thing*, as in a computer program designed to take note of my woes before I do), rebooked the flight, got me first on stand-by, and later confirmed a seat—all while I was in a meeting. As I was headed to the airport going through my voice-mail messages, I heard the entire headache being resolved—by someone else, without my involvement. First, there was the call at 1:15 alerting me to the flight cancellation; then, the call at 1:32 telling me I was on stand-by for another flight; then, the call at 1:47 explaining that I now had a confirmed seat. Real people, really involved. I got home. This was an example of tremendous risk reduction, which I can personally compare to booking a flight directly with United—another passion brand moment, but the passion was raw fury.

Again, an absolutely true tale: Mattie and I were flying to

Crested Butte for a ski vacation with her great friend Olivia and my great friend Serra, Oliva's mother. It's a Friday late afternoon. We couldn't fly together with them because Mattie was in a performance of *Macbeth* given by her second-grade class, so we are going later.

We catch the United flight to Denver with no hitch, but there's the connecting flight to the airport nearest our final destination, Crested Butte. We get to Denver in time, arrive at the appointed gate, and wait, and wait, and wait. Nobody tells us anything, except that the flight will be taking off on time. Still we sit. Then they start boarding and stop boarding; the rumor is that the air-conditioning doesn't work. It's March in Colorado. We probably won't need it, but still. We sit there. It's 8:30. It's 9:15. It's 9:59. Someone informs us that if we can't take off by 10 p.m., we can't go, because the airport we're flying into won't accept a landing after 10:30, or some such.

At 10 p.m. at night they cancel the flight. At 10:30 they tell us that if we've checked luggage we can go downstairs to collect it—best guess is that it will be there by 2 a.m. They also tell us that they will put us on the next available flight, which—because this is spring ski season after all—is the next Monday at 1 p.m. They also inform us that if we're thinking about renting a car and driving, Hertz closes at 10 p.m. They will put us up for one night in a local hotel. This is the news, parceled out one-on-one as the line of tired, angry travelers snakes through the gate area where one lone United representative irritably dismisses every plea for leniency or even common sense.

I catch a young fellow's eye. He's asking a friend, "Should we try to rent a car and drive there?" I interject myself into the equation. Yes! I don't quite believe that Hertz closes at the Denver airport at 10 p.m., so I call them and, indeed, they have a car for us. Only one guy wants to drive with Mattie and me, so we strike a deal. I'll start. We'll take turns. And we do, with Mattie in the backseat, sound asleep. It's about midnight when we get on the road. We drive up the Rockies through a pass that's closed to truckers. There is no other traffic and it's snowing lightly. We get lost once, which adds another hour to the route. I drop him off at the airport and drive on the next thirty-five miles to Crested Butte. We get to the hotel at 6:30 a.m.

The vacation returns to normal, after a bit of sleep. Our luggage is delivered to the airport and I have to drive there the next day to retrieve it. When we get back to New York, I take the unused ticket for the cancelled flight and mail it with a letter to United Customer Service, asking them to refund the money. I'm still waiting for an answer.

So there you have it. Orbitz may look like the disintermediator of airline travel, requiring me to coproduce my itinerary, but rather it's become a terrific intermediary. United, which was once one of the world's premiere airlines, is in my experience one step above Greyhound. The social *and* performance *and* financial *and* time risks are actually higher with the big brand. The rewards arrive from the savvy start-up.

Third comes the *cost-benefit analysis phase*. We factor in the costs (economic, psychological, social) of becoming involved in coproduction with a brand versus our assessment of the rewards. I may want to remodel my kitchen, but once I really, really think about it, I have to admit it's probably going to be a major mess, doubtlessly involving scores of professionals to clean up after me and set the counter level. Some tasks are beyond us. Others, perhaps like creating a photo book on Shutterfly.com, seem well worth the agitation of acquiring a new series of skills. Digital photography in general is indeed an excellent example of coproduction.

The fourth stage is *deciding to engage*. This can be the

Mine the Mythos. The basic Camel Lights pack carries with it the familiar camel, the typeface, the palette, the heritage mark "since 1913" and the "Turkish domestic blend" descriptor that have been essential elements of the brand's promise for nearly a century. Taken together, they badge the smoker's choice as authentic — if not mainstream.

Work the Worldview. The ads that launched Chemistry.com made clear the inclusive promise of Chemistry versus the prior experience of many singles rejected by eHarmony.

Was it my hobbies? If you've been rejected by eHarmony, don't feel bad. Millions of people looking for love have been. At Chemistry.com, those diverse, keep-you-on-your-toes people are just who we're looking for. The ones you'd actually want to share a life—and a bed—with. See what our chemistry-inspired matches can do for you. **Your first five are free. Visit Chemistry.com today.**

NEW!
chemistry.com™
COME AS YOU ARE™

S.B.D.G.

**NO GAYS
ON BEACH
MAY-SEPT**

Did you do a double take when you saw this sign? You might have the same reaction when you learn that eHarmony doesn't accept gays. At Chemistry.com, we're not here to judge, just to ignite. Whether you're gay or straight, we believe everyone deserves the kind of love that makes you go weak in the knees. See what our chemistry-inspired matches can do for you. **Your first five are free. Visit Chemistry.com today.**

chemistry.com
COME AS YOU ARE™

Brand the Buzz. Then, Chemistry moved the dialogue up a notch to challenge the philosophy undergirding eHarmony, sparking potent word of mouth in real time and online.

eHarmony's founder preaches that premarital sex can "cloud decisions." What is this, 1952? At Chemistry.com we don't tell you who, when or how to love. Our job is simply to light the fire. See what our chemistry-inspired matches can do for you. **Your first five are free. Check into Chemistry.com today.**

chemistry.com™
COME AS YOU ARE™

Differentiate on Design. Not your usual gym ad, this one brings wit and an irreverent sensibility, as well as use of nontraditional media, to take the Crunch argument to the streets and the urinals.

island

Know they know you need them. The Island campaign spoke right to traders through media they'd see on the way to work and home, in the authoritative and legitimizing voice more usually used for consumer brands: You matter.

Hire Passionistas. The founders of the company were the ad and PR guys behind the campaign. A labor of love, Tappening has grown because of the urgency of their (and their company's employees') belief that what they can do right now can make a difference forever.

actual purchase at IKEA of a bed, sofa, or table. It could be the moment I log onto Fidelity and decide to be my own investment broker. It could be the moment I go to M&M.com and buy customized candy for Mattie's birthday favors. Perhaps it's when I summon the courage to edit an entry at Wikipedia.org. Or when I move to online banking. Or when I agree to go with Mattie to Build-a-Bear-Workshop and watch her participate in coproduction. It seems worth it. It seems possible. It seems like a bit of adventure. Even fun. It's the moment of actualization.

Finally, we enter the *Was it worth it? phase*. Typically, we compare and contrast to real-world alternatives, such as going to Macy's furniture department, meeting with a broker, or trying to find interesting party favors. But increasingly, we have other virtual competitors with which to compare. Is this one as easy as that one? The barriers to switching become the new hurdles. Just because somebody tells me about a much more intuitive investment Web site with much lower fees, does that mean I really want to move my Fidelity account or change banks?

Coproduction seems like a fact of life by now. We're not so amazed and delighted by it as we once were. Remember the first time you used an ATM and didn't have to wait in line before 2 p.m. on a Friday to get enough money for the weekend? Probably not, but it happened. And the tellers weren't any happier to be there than we were.

THE THIRD RING: COMARKETING

Beyond coproduction, however, comes the next rung of the brand democracy ladder: comarketing. "Our customers tend to be creative and we've given them the biggest canvas we have to express themselves—our advertising," says Erik Soderstrom, director of global brand development for Converse shoes.[3] But he's talking about giving over the marketing reins for just a very short time, which, oddly enough, are the easiest to share, compared to product design or brand expansion.

The industry trade press is packed with news of brands, like Frito-Lay, Tide, and Converse, which seek to channel brand excitement into new approaches to marketing. One recent article takes it a bit farther with "P&G Lets Consumers Act as Media Planners."

Consumers are remarkably willing to enlist in their favorite brand's marketing army; that much is clear. When Mt. Olive Pickles, a regional Southern brand, wanted to launch its lunchbox snack pack, it developed a "Name the PicklePAK" promotion. More than fifty thousand consumers submitted names for the four-member PicklePAK "spokespickles."

Do such ventures simply show that we consumers have too much time on our hands? Perhaps. But something at work here suggests a real desire for consumer participation in brand development. Most often it is seen in such promotions, but surely there are larger opportunities.

The race is on to get consumers to create, to produce, to actively participate in the marketing, instead of passively watching or listening. One consultant terms this the consumer's movement from "deferential to referential." No longer in awe of a brand or its advertising, we use key brands as badges to market ourselves.

If by brand democracy we mean marketing partner, then Converse and others have taken the lead here. Converse has asked the general public to offer film, artwork, and music to use in its ads for the Chuck Taylor shoe, offering a ten-thousand-dollar prize, plus airtime for the best film, with a thousand-dollar prize for any entry used on its Web site.

The starting premise? "Taglines Are Evil," according to

John Butler of Butler, Shine, Stern and Partners, the ad agency representing Converse, presumably in an effort to allay or at least acknowledge an ambient mistrust of three clever words masquerading as an appealing truth. But, of course, what is "Taglines Are Evil," but a tagline?

The offer? Tell the story in twenty-four seconds. The agency spread the news of the contest through posters, ads in design and film schools, in *Juxtapoz* magazine, and by word of mouth. The response? Fifteen hundred short films.

Along with the creative outpouring arrived other indicators of democracy: An outcry against unfair practices, payments, and treatment of these lay creatives, augmented by professional derision of the agency for having abdicated its role in marketing the product. (See pp. 161–63)

Many consumer products companies have opted for these "send in your commercial" promotions, riffing on the excitement of reality television and contest programs like *American Idol*. Even the usually staid business-to-business, financial sector has worked this angle, as with the Island ECN (the trader's trading company) campaign, in support of a genuine David in a land of financial Goliaths.

Its agency, DiMassimo Goldstein, worked hand in hand with Island to reorient the company away from making claims of superior liquidity in this complex, confusing, and narrow market of financial trading action. Rather, Island was positioned to the customer as the "Trader's Marketplace." The financial traders themselves were celebrated as heroic, in dramatic fashion: customer as star of the show.

The company came to understand that traders typically view themselves as the top-gun fighter pilots of the financial markets. So, DiMassimo Goldstein hired *Top Gun* movie director Tony Scott to help articulate the traders' inner and outer life for a series of spots that ran on CNBC, over stock market trading floors everywhere. This identity and celebration of individual traders was rewarded; within nine months Island had not only closed the gap with former leader Instinet, but had decisively taken possession of the number one spot. Some days more than 30 percent of the NASDAQ was traded on Island.

The brand touched the traders in real time with bar programs and promotions to celebrate their successes. Island gained continuing insight into how to best advance the campaign, and even shared a few custom-made beverages, including the Deep Liquitini and the Closing Bellini. The ongoing truth of the campaign for its creators: It's not our liquidity; it's the traders' liquidity that matters.

But ultimately, consumers and customers who act as marketing partners are not sufficient proof of brand democracy. When Converse's Soderstrom speaks of handing over the reins of the brand, he is handing them to people passionate about marketing more than athletic shoes. After all, the Chuck Taylor promotion was targeted to art students, not gym rats.

While I applaud and many times enjoy these efforts at marketing engagement, I believe it's just the beginning of what brand democratization will ultimately come to mean. Of course, it's interesting to have consumers show off their marketing and technology skills. It fits with the insights in chapter 5, "Know They Know You Need Them." Still, a passion for marketing is a far cry from passion for the brand itself. As a way of thinking about brand democracy, one study puts it this way: "Someone said to me . . . you're no longer brand manager, you're brand bystander."[4]

HITTING THE BULL'S-EYE: BRAND CONSUMER PARTNERSHIP

Is the benefit of brand democracy solely to develop the brand personality—or the brand itself?

The people who use your brand are well qualified to help chart its fortune, telling you what they want and how they want it. The brand's job is to be responsive, like a friend or a mate. Great brands are making the effort with the tactics at hand, but it's much easier if the brand is Internet based rather than sold at the corner store.

Brand democratization as I mean it is best represented by business models that require the active participation of consumers to drive, mold, and design the product. Think of eBay, *American Idol,* and nearly any social networking site.

The world of social networking can be said to have launched on the Web in 1997 with Sixdegrees.com, which shut down in 2000. That period saw the entrance of scores of comparable, yet quite specific sites: AsianAvenue, BlackPlanet, MiGente, LiveJournal, Cyworld (Korean), and LunarStorm (Swedish). Ryze.com was launched in 2001 to help establish and maintain business networks, followed by Tribe.net, Friendster, and LinkedIn. MySpace started in 2003.

Facebook was created in 2004 and three years later had 21 million registered members, generating 1.6 billion page views each day. The typical member spends about twenty minutes a day on the site, and two-thirds of the users log in at least once a day. Originally designed for college students, the high school version was launched in 2005. The next year, the company introduced communities for organizations, with about twenty-two thousand signing up within a year. It had become the seventh most popular site on the World Wide Web.

These types of sites are particularly adroit at helping participants gain and leverage social capital, the assets that accrue to members because they are involved in a strong community. If you're good at math and I'm not and I have a required math class I'm worried about, my connection to you through Facebook is a piece of social capital I can leverage. Although the promise of such sites was to allow people to meet friends of friends, they are usually used most easily to maintain relationships initially created off-line, reducing the traditional barriers of time and effort involved. In other words, these sites are used to keep in touch with contacts made elsewhere rather than those initiated online.

These are brands engineered to morph dynamically into new versions of themselves *because* consumers interact with them. Digg.com is another: "A place for people to discover and share content from anywhere on the web." Flickr.com is another, self-proclaimed "almost certainly the best online photo management and sharing application in the world."

I believe that Wikipedia is probably the best illustration of a democratic brand, with all the ups and downs that entails. It has termed itself the free encyclopedia, taking its name from the notion of a portmanteau—a combination of words and meanings—as in wiki, a type of communal Web site, and encyclopedia. It started as a subsidiary of Nupedia, which in turn collapsed under the weight of trying to become a free old-media encyclopedia. Wikipedia was left standing and now is written by volunteers from throughout the world, collaborating to make a reference site that welcomes nearly 700 million visitors a year. There are roughly 75,000 active contributors working on 10 million articles in more than 250 languages.

Anyone can contribute, but there are rules. Mostly the rules tell us what Wikipedia is *not*. To wit, quoting directly from the Web site:

Wikipedia is not a dictionary.
Wikipedia is not a publisher of original thought.
Wikipedia is not a soapbox.
Wikipedia is not a mirror or a repository of links, images, or media files.
Wikipedia is not a blog, webspace provider, social networking, or memorial site.
Wikipedia is not a directory.
Wikipedia is not a manual, guidebook, or textbook.
Wikipedia is not a crystal ball.
Wikipedia is not an indiscriminate collection of information.
Wikipedia is not censored.
Wikipedia is not a democracy.
Wikipedia is not a bureaucracy.
Wikipedia is not a battleground.
Wikipedia is not an anarchy.
Wikipedia is not your web host.[5]

The Wikipedia policy for articles is to have a neutral point of view, to be verifiable, and to offer no original research. From a collaborative perspective, it asks its contributors to work with civility, seek consensus, shun personal attacks, look for dispute resolution, and not make legal threats.

What's particularly fascinating to me is the raw transparency of the site, which explains that it is a nonprofit charitable organization founded in St. Petersburg, Florida, in 2002 and headquartered in San Francisco. So far so good. Then comes this really remarkable background of employees:

The functions of the Wikimedia Foundation were, for the first few years, executed almost entirely by volunteers. In the spring of 2005, the foundation only had two employees, Danny Wool and Brion Vibber. Though the number of employees has grown, the bulk of foundation work continues to be done by volunteers, with the foundation having very few employees.

On June 16, 2006, Brad Patrick, previously a practicing attorney who had done some pro bono work with the foundation starting in fall 2005, was named general counsel and interim executive director; in the latter capacity, Patrick was designated to assist the board in its search for a permanent executive director.

As of October 4, 2006, the Wikimedia Foundation had five paid employees: two programmers (software manager Brion Vibber in California and server administrator Chad Perrin in Tampa); "to answer the phones," administrative assistant Barbara Brown; to handle fundraising and grants, Danny Wool; and to manage, interim executive director Brad Patrick.

As of December 8, 2006, the Wikimedia Foundation's list of current staff named three other technical independent contractors (part-time hardware manager Kyle Anderson in Tampa, full-time MediaWiki software developer Tim Starling, and part-time networking coordinator Mark Bergsma).

Brad Patrick ceased his activity as interim director in January 2007 and then resigned from his position as legal counsel in April 2007.

In January 2007, Carolyn Doran was named Chief Operating Officer and Sandy Ordonez came on board as Communication Manager. Doran had begun working as a part-time bookkeeper for the foundation in 2006 after being sent by a temporary agency.

Danny Wool, officially the grant coordinator but also largely involved in fundraising and business development, resigned in March 2007. In April 2007, the foundation added a new position, Chapter Coordinator, and appointed Delphine Ménard, then in the position of Volunteer Coordinator, to fill it. Cary Bass was appointed to replace Ménard.

In May 2007, Vishal Patel was hired to assist in business development.

In July 2007, Mike Godwin was hired as general counsel and legal coordinator. That same month, Carolyn Doran left as COO and Sue Gardner was hired as consultant and special advisor. The number of full-time staff members, after these hires, was still fewer than ten.

In December 2007, it was revealed by *The Register* that former COO Carolyn Doran was a convicted felon, with a DUI arrest during her tenure at the Foundation and a substantial criminal history, including shooting her boyfriend and charges of complicity in credit card forgery.[6]

I cannot imagine any major corporation being willing to share the bad with the good so straightforwardly. There is a lot of chat about the importance of transparency in a brand—or, indeed, any democracy. But we rarely witness it as starkly as in this example.

Threadless.com is a different case, operating via a Web site but making an oftentimes commoditized physical product. It's a T-shirt company that manufacturers designs submitted and selected by consumers. This is a fascinating consumer community that is viewed by many as a harbinger of the movement away from passive consumerism. It has allowed the company to become what the consumers want it to be and that includes growing beyond an online presence to establish retail settings, as well as introducing children's clothing, prints, and posters.

A cursory review of the Threadless Web site shows a brand eager to engage: Grab our RSS feed; Join our Facebook group; Follow us on Twitter; Make us your Flickr contact; Be our MySpace Friend. New tees and prints are unveiled every Monday, as the site explains, "With the help of our community, we select and print hundreds of amazing new designs each year, awarding over one million dollars to artists around the world."[7]

Some of the designs: A yellow shirt with the saying "Being

vague is almost as fun as doing this other thing"; a purple one saying "Technology Ruins Nature"; or a white shirt saying "Stupid raisins, stay out of my cookies" in a brown circle. Another brand run by the same company is Naked & Angry, set to launch handbags and dinnerware, designed by and "elected" for manufacturing by consumers.

Another tiny entrant that begins to suggest where we may be headed: Nvohk (pronounced invoke) is a fashion company that is introducing a "collective customer commitment" model. The goal is to get five thousand members to buy in with fifty dollars each, use the money to design eco-friendly clothes, sell the clothes to the public at large, and share the profits with the original investors. The fifty-dollar fee includes the right to vote on new designs and weigh in on business decisions.

Although it's easier to see this type of brand participation via the Internet or on reality television, my high school buddy Tim Harper, a journalist, author, and educator, started his own publishing company to allow writers to tell their stories directly, without the intermediaries of agents, publishing houses, and bricks and mortar retailers. Books By Bookends takes the manuscript in a Word document, transforms it into a bound volume, gets the ISBN, and arranges for it to be posted on Amazon. After that, it sells or doesn't, based on the author's talent, marketing savvy, and tenacity.

A study in Britain by the Marketing Society says that we are moving from a "down load" society to an "up load" society in which "the enlightened belief is that this will have a fundamental impact on brands and traditional methods of brand building and management will cease to be relevant." While I'm dubious about management ceasing to be relevant, I am in agreement with the demise of traditional brand building. One interviewee in the study says, "Brands in the future will have to engage more with the consumer and be open and confident enough to have that engagement . . . [including] the brand being shaped by the consumer."[8]

When M&M Mars announced it would make customized M&Ms with personal inscriptions in a wide variety of colors via a Web site, nearly everyone I knew in the confections business scoffed. "They can't make money at it!" was one cry. "Consumers won't spend that much!" was the other. Indeed, at twelve dollars a bag with a three-bag minimum, M&Ms suddenly started to look pretty upscale. But from that initial foray, the M&Ms site has expanded to include birthday, Chanukah, business, Christmas, and wedding celebration options, bringing the total to eighty-five dollars and more for twenty bags, boxes, or cut-glass containers. Obviously the brand has tapped into an unmet need—and it did it with an easy to navigate, entertaining process that allows not just personalized messages but an appealing palate of candy colors found nowhere else.

Indeed, the ability of a brand to offer some sort of customization is one of the hallmarks of a brand democracy. The Consumed column of the *New York Times Magazine* reported on "earphone identity" as a means of expression, a "compulsion to personalize inanimate objects."

Another indicator of giving over the reins to consumers, at least provisionally, is illustrated by the Wispa campaign on Facebook. This was not a marketing campaign targeting consumers, but rather one that targeted the manufacturer, Cadbury Schweppes, which had discontinued making Wispa, a UK chocolate bar. Fourteen thousand Brits reportedly joined the "bring back Wispa" movement and the company relented, offering to make 23 million bars, enough to test the water and ensure that this groundswell demand wasn't just a "joke that snowballed."

* * *

A great example of the consumer engagement vision in action is Google. "This brand was built intentionally, person by person, through the actions of millions of people in a personalized setting and then reinforced by those people talking to each other," explains John Battelle, author of *The Search: How Google and Its Rivals Rewrote the Rules of Business and Transformed Our Culture*.[9] The model toward which we are moving harnesses real people, not employees of the company, who adapt products to their needs and desires then share their adaptations with friends, family, and colleagues.

The Google model, which is essentially a network model, making its money from advertisers' willingness to exchange money for eyeballs, is a dynamic one. An article in the *New York Times* by Miguel Helft makes the obsession to detail obvious. "If Google were the United States government, the data that streams onto Nicholas Fox's laptop every day would be classified as top secret. The number of searches and clicks, the rate at which users click on ads, the revenue this generates—everything is tracked hour by hour, compared with the data from a week earlier and charted. His group's mission to constantly fine-tune Google's ad delivery system has one overriding objective: Show users only the ads they are most likely to be interested in and click on."[10]

Now that is a brand democracy model. The goals of the company and the consumer are mightily aligned. It wants the same thing we want and its financial health depends upon its ability to pay attention. One of the unpredictable benefits of this type of democracy is that, according to a 2008 Harris Poll, Google is now viewed as the "most reputable company" in America. A Harris Poll spokesperson explained, "Google is the perfect example showing reputation does not correlate with ad spending. The positive perception of how you treat your employees, your corporate-social responsibility efforts, and your products and services and the amount of media (these factors) can generate probably trumps any ad spend they would ever want to make."[11]

According to Gary Hamel's *The Future of Management*, "What makes Google unique is less its Web-centric business model, but rather its brink-of-chaos management model. Key components include a wafer-thin hierarchy, a dense network of lateral communication, a policy of giving outsized rewards to people who come up with outsized ideas, a team-focused approach to product development, and a corporate credo that challenges every employee to *put the user first*."[12]

Another example of bringing the voice of the consumer to the table directly is my own favorite, Fresh Direct. When consumers balked at the number and size of cardboard boxes used to deliver its wares, the company began using boxes more appropriately sized to contents (no more huge box housing a single quart of milk) and converted to using 100 percent post-consumer material for its boxes. It's also gone the additional environmentally conscious steps of using recycled paper for promotional flyers, biodiesel fuel in its delivery trucks, and sustainable food wherever it can. Fresh Direct partnered with City Harvest to make sure that foods not sold go to organizations that help feed low-income families. It works with Bright Power energy consultants to redesign the warehouse facility's lighting system, using brighter, more-energy-efficient fixtures and bulbs.

Beyond this, the company seems to work ceaselessly to keep the offerings interesting, ensuring that shopping with Freshdirect.com is always a fresh experience, never the rote endeavor of a conventional grocery. In its arsenal are some fabulous offerings including artisanal cheeses, Montauk Day-boat lobsters, mussels and clams, enticing catering feasts for ten to a hundred, and chef-prepared appetizers and entrees from well-known local restaurants. Its line of four-minute meals proves that convenience need not come at the expense of flavor and fun.

The service seems almost profligate with new ideas. Some work, others don't, as voted on by the pocketbooks of its consumers. A democratically governed country doesn't decide *everything* by majority rule, but rather through representation. As Fresh Direct makes clear, the markers of genuine brand democracy must certainly include the consumer/customer as stakeholder while also involving other partners, such as suppliers, farmers, chefs, and other artisans, led by the passionate advocacy of its chief executive officer. Equally, since this firm was started as an entirely new model, not the offshoot of an existing grocery chain, Wall Street and the investment community were crucial. The development of internal competencies, such as finance, sales, distribution, marketing, and strategic alliances, were all begun and refined as the company grew.

In an article in the *Atlantic*, Corby Kummer writes, "The expenses and risks of setting up an online company that ships fresh produce are exceptionally high—so high that Webvan, the most ambitious of the start-ups that set out to do this on a national scale, lost $830 million and went bankrupt before delivering a single box on the East Coast."[13]

Fresh Direct made some better choices, including keeping the delivery zone modest—just key areas of New York City to begin—and ensuring a two-hour window of next-day delivery rather than Webvan's pledged half hour. They also benefited from being able to buy Webvan's equipment and vans at highly discounted prices.

As Kummer describes it, the Fresh Direct warehouse and order center rivals a visit to Hershey Park. "Order baskets travel on elevated hooks from one part of the plant to another; bags of beets whiz down wheeled conveyor platforms to a box waiting on a sort of trolley track ready to go to the deli department. The whole system—from kitchen to cheese room to butcher and fish cutter to dry-goods area—looks like a miniature ride in a food theme park, with neat cardboard boxes instead of, say, giant teacups."

We'll have to take his word for it, since the entire system is off limits. Fresh Direct reportedly spent $100 million to create it and, while imitation may be the sincerest form of flattery, so far replicating its process has been a tremendous barrier to entry for would-be competitors.

Getting the voice of the consumer at the conference room table may be a significant challenge, but in the intricate and often politically charged balancing acts within the modern corporation it is just one of many challenges to brand dynamism. Seen from a passion brand perspective, Fresh Direct was lucky to have been a start-up with no entrenched corporate animosities grandfathered into the equation and everyone working with the passion of the pioneer, redefining a stodgy industry.

This model illustrates how I believe passion brands must evolve and grow, with a nearly obsessive commitment to those who are excited by the category—both internal corporate audience and external customer audiences, crucial stakeholders in the financial markets, supply and distribution systems, and our advocates and adversaries.

THE PASSION MODEL

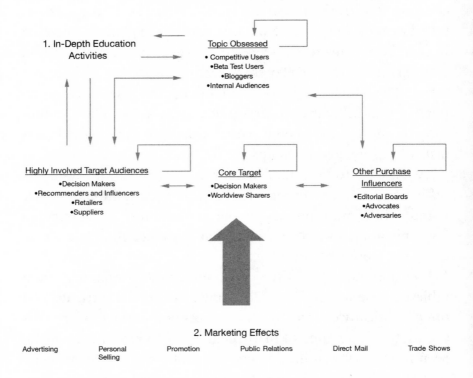

It's always hard to find the future in the present. The best place currently to see this level of brand engagement in action is in the online community at Second Life, the brainchild of Philip Rosedale, president of Linden Research. It is not, as the entry on Wikipedia is quick to point out, a game. "It does not have points, scores, winners or losers, levels, an end-strategy or most of the other characteristics of games." What it did have, as of March 2008, was approximately 13 million accounts, with an estimated usage by "residents" of 28 million hours, with about 38,000 logged on at any one time.

To join, residents create an avatar, an online persona that may or may very well not be at all like themselves. Second Life's economy is based on the Linden Dollar (L$). As in the real world, currency is volatile, but in February 2007 the exchange rate was L$266 to one US dollar. Residents buy land in US$ ranging from $5 to $195 a month.

The wall separating the real from virtual world is increasingly opaque. The Maldives was the first country to open an embassy in Second Life; Sweden, Estonia, and Israel followed. Reuters maintains a bureau in Second Life. *Gossip Girl*, the CW network TV show, films "machinisodes" inside Second Life. Yes, of course, it's not a physical place: it's a physical space within the virtual world.

I first learned of this community in a 2006 e-mail from Adam Hanft, the fellow who runs the ad agency that created Chemistry.com. The e-mail's headline: "How's this for consumer generated content?" He was alerting me to Starwood's decision to open a virtual version of a new line of hotels before breaking ground on its inns. The virtual hotels would open in Second Life.

The concept for Starwood, Hanft wrote, was "to glean enough valuable data from the way online avatars react to the new hotel to help shape the one being constructed on Planet Earth." And now, more than two years later, a new chain of hotels has opened: Aloft, from Starwood, with a contemporary design informed by the interaction between the hotel prototype and Second Life avatars.

This to me seems like a brand democracy hybrid: using the virtual world to engage consumers in deciding how a real-world brand should evolve. Brands have to sit up and take notice. When one of Second Life's denizens created an online version of the IKEA catalog to help new arrivals decorate their digital homes, IKEA didn't sue. It created its own cyberstore based on competitor *The Sims 2* from Electronic Arts, where participants can buy "stuff packs" from H&M or IKEA, and major brands like Philips, Electrolux, Sony, Starbucks,

Dunkin' Donuts, Pepsi, Coca-Cola, and Borders books are all in negotiation to claim some prime town-center real estate when *Sims 3* debuts in 2009.

To the extent these brands view Second Life and its parallel universe competitors as simple advertising buys, the opportunity to create genuine brand democracies will be deferred a bit longer, while what they gain is just another billboard. The much larger opportunity is to engage in these universes in order to learn, to try, to fail, and to learn some more about how real people really want their passion brands to respond to them.

When Aloft originally said that its check-in time would be 4 p.m. and check-out would be 10 a.m., consumers rebelled. Some bloggers speculated that Starwood had promised investors it could make a successful business that could charge an average of $150 a night by employing fewer cleaning personnel but give them two additional hours of clean-up time. When the Aloft chain started taking reservations for its real hotels, the check-out time posted was noon. It had quickly learned in the virtual world and made the consumer-driven revision.

THE FREE PRESS OF A BRAND DEMOCRACY
Speak Up, A Division of Under Consideration
In response to a Glowing Report of Converse's "Brand Democracy" Campaign,
which it termed "Inspired" and referenced Converse as a
Peggy Guggenheim–like patron of the arts

Inspired? . . . not really . . .

I'm calling bullshit on this one. Converse is not a "patron of the arts" in this case. Converse has become the beneficiary. Let's examine this "Brand Democracy" and the reality of what Converse owns and does not own. Found in one of the 11 forms you must include with submission: By submitting the Film and any other material, you agree to transfer, and transfer any and all of your right, title and interest in and to the Film, including but not limited to any and all copyrights, trademark rights, "moral rights" and any and all other rights that may exist, throughout the world, to Converse.

I think they make it pretty clear who OWNS Converse, the Chuck Taylor brand and now your creative work.

Further they can make derivative works of your submission with permission . . .

Say what you will about this being fun, an opportunity, chance for exposure, possibility of making $10K. But, Converse is effectively "commissioning artists" to create original art that promotes their brand with no guarantee of remuneration for that art and then claiming rights to it.

Sorry, but you lost. In case you did not understand how much you lost, you just legally gave up the right to show the work as your own. So forget posting it on your site or using it on your reel to promote your abilities. This company—now owned by Nike (2004)—that is the year following its Chapter 11 bankruptcy filing posted revenue of $205 million.

As for "Brand Democracy," well, that part is correct. But not in the idealistic definition we attach to the word—where the People decide who is worthy. It is more in keeping with the "control of an organization or group by the majority of its members," meaning You the People do not decide who is worthy of this honor. It is the agency and Converse.

As for BS&S and other agencies "turning the creating over to the public" and farming "consumer generated content" and cloaking it behind pallid veneer of "brand democracy" is disheartening. I think it's "brand laziness."

Would BS&S have created 1500 :30's for such a paltry sum? How much are they getting paid for coming up with the "idea?" I hope it's a lot because they deserve it. Seriously, they garnered 1500 pieces of creative for their client for under a $million? (NOTE: The Converse site has approximately 69 "films" in the gallery.) That's brilliant and they should be paid fairly, if not handsomely.

Now we are seeing a rise of "consumer evangelism" as people embrace and champion their own brand endorsement as a vehicle for self-expression.

Converse, like many other large 'hip' companies are really getting stuck into the 'user created content' idea of promotion. I know 'user created content' is normally game oriented—but isn't this one big game? I fully think . . . is right—this isn't about being democratic, it's about being lazy. Any good creative should be "good' enough to know that the winner of this Converse competition wanted to see—hence what they made themselves. The challenge is for designers and creative to achieve this for ourselves and not become lazy . . .

My feeling is that younger creatives these days are more willing to just do things for the heck of it, for bragging rights, for the 15 seconds of fame (15 minutes is now way too much). With sites like Flickr and YouTube "things" (videos, photos, illustrations) are just up there on the internet with little credit of the creator. "Things" are up for swiping all the time . . .

I'm not defending Converse, but at the same time I don't think people are poor, defenseless, uneducated victims . . .

This was a spec campaign, pure and simple. Converse can dress it up in a toga all they want, but it's still spec. And it still damages the industry as a result. It is an unfortunately common practice that commercial production companies will often pay to produce spec spots for their directors in order to keep their reel fresh and associate them with a 'hip' brand. I hope it pays off . . .

Converse exploits people for their creativity. People exploit Converse for their vanity . . .

The harm is that it devalues the work you do for a living and makes people think they can get design (or directing, as the case may be) for free.

There are ways—I think the Converse is one of them—in which you can involve the public without the ulterior motive of screwing people and being corporationey.

Yes, I now kick it high-style in the Bahamas every other weekend with the proceeds of the poster contest! Suckers!

WHAT WE TALK ABOUT WHEN WE TALK ABOUT BRANDS

Democratize the Brand

Verbatim Consumer Quotes

"You know the really great thing about crackers is that they are always there for you. They are the ultimate convenience food. Everybody has a box in the cupboard—or they are easy enough to run out and get at the deli—and some cheese and a bottle of wine and you can have friends over. It's pretty cool. And, when you're hungover, crackers help that too. I have a special recipe for saltines and soda and pretty soon I'm feeling perky. Plus, you can always crunch them up in soup. My grandma taught me that. I can see her now. I was just a kid. I was hungry and she gave me soup and crackers and showed me how to crumble them into the soup. It was our thing. They let you do stuff. Pretty cool really. People don't think about it like that, but it's true."

"So I wrote to them with this really, really great idea. It could have been huge. I didn't want money. I just wanted them to use my idea. It would have been so cool. Everybody I told about it thought it'd be great, man. But, I got some dumb form letter back from a legal type. They hadn't even read my idea, afraid I'd sue them or something stupid like that. I just wanted to be the guy who showed them how to do this with their product, but no. Couldn't do that. Nope."

"It's absolutely the coolest thing. You go in and you push some buttons and out comes the exact sandwich you want, I mean exact. The kind of bread, the kind of meat, cheese, whatever, mustard, no mustard. All exactly the way you want it, like from a robot. I mean I guess there's somebody back there who's doing it, but you don't deal with them. It's kind of your construction project. You design it. You might feel weird telling some counter guy that you want mustard, mayo, AND ketchup on your turkey, ham, and Swiss on pumpernickel, with some sauerkraut and pickles. I mean it sounds like you're way too into your sandwich, right? But here, with this machine, it's like it's custom made. It's cool."

"My friends tell me I'm creative, so I do sometimes try to enter those contests they have, right? Some brands. It's just fun. Like to put something together for MySpace or something like that. Facebook. It's just fun. Fun to play at marketing. I mean who cares if you win or not, it's just something to do and to show people. They get a kick out of it. I mean it would be cool to have something you did appear on television, but that's a long shot, right? A real long shot. It's mostly for the fun of it and to have something to get really into, you know. I mean your head gets really into how are you going to show how cool this brand is, what could make it really fun and cool and that kind of thing, but not trying too hard. Like a cool brand. How do you do that? It's interesting to me. I like looking at what other people do, too. Like seeing how they solve the puzzle. That kind of thing."

Chapter 7
MINE THE MYTHOS

F Scott Fitzgerald wrote in *The Great Gatsby* that personality is forged by an "unbroken string of successful small gestures." As with people, so with brands. Brand personality takes root in the soil of its own heritage and history. Some brands have to make up a past. Others have ancestry galore to properly utilize if the brand's stewards can find the right tone to strike without relying too much on pure nostalgia, thereby foregoing the relevance to today that any great brand needs. I'm calling this the brand's mythos—the backstory that is archetypally true, the mythic legend of itself told to itself and its fans.

The rule here is to "remember" but not to be slavishly tethered to mythos. Crest started out life as a cavity-preventing toothpaste, but it's grown and evolved into an "oral care system" with whitening, tartar control, breath freshener, and a host of other related benefits that appeal to nearly every age and stage. It's a fine line to walk, the organic trajectory of the brand's DNA, staying within a logic that consumers can follow

BRANDING PROCESS STEP 6

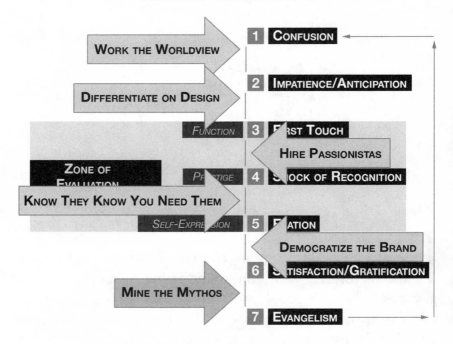

and the bounds of believability, while allowing the brand to be alive, vital, and delighting. So we honor the brand's past, without getting stuck in it.

Think about the Mini Cooper cars. "The Mini Cooper played the nostalgia card gracefully," one Ford exec tells me. "It was a forty-year-old brand brought back in 2000, with a design that echoed the racy 1961 original: the scooped head-lights, recessed door handles, chunky wheels, and box aes-thetic paying authentic homage without trying to be old in a new setting. Inspired by, rather than a direct replica."[1]

Car aficionados can articulate the five critical components of the Mini Cooper's success: the car's parentage brings quality assurance; the racy performance and road handling adds expe-riential sizzle; its interior appointments suggest compelling thoughtfulness; its distinctive design screams *Pay Attention To Me!*; and its buzzworthy marketing (more about this in a moment) says you're not dealing with just another vehicle, but an attitude, a worldview that includes large dashes of wit.

Even the experts didn't realize what a phenomenon it would become. At the 2000 Auto Show in Detroit it was derided. In 2002, it was the car of the year, with sales of 125,000, up 25 percent over its target.

Even more impressive, really, is its success in Japan, arguably the birthplace of the compact car. The Japanese buy nearly one-quarter of all the Minis produced. When it came time to launch the Mini Cooper, Rover took back management of the brand in Japan and made two essential decisions: first, a commitment to supporting the Mini in Japan, buying back the import franchise and making unique modifications to the Mini Cooper required by Japanese regulations; second, straightforwardly linking it to its Rover heritage, a step not taken elsewhere in the global markets. Because of the perceived appeal for the Japanese of this storied birthright, the car created what the designers called a balanced reciprocity between the Rover and Mini Cooper mark.

"The Mini Cooper's attraction is not primarily at the functionally-tangible level but at an iconically intangible level," write Stuart Laverick and Kevin Johnston in the industry journal *Marketing Intelligence & Planning*. "The Mini Cooper, like all icons, is the manifestation of a sentiment—culture made flesh—and a rich representation of a vastly image-rich period in British culture."[2]

The Mini Cooper then offered Japanese drivers "genuine Britishness, traditional design, traditional materials and, perhaps most importantly, the opportunity to personalize their purchase and stand out from the crowd," according to Nicki Darzinskas, a small car brand manager at Rover.[3] Notice that in the United States the appeal was one of a basic, small economy car with an idiosyncratic attitude. The Rover name would have limited, not advanced, the story here.

This entire notion of the iconic tug of brands is worth dwelling on for a bit. The writer defines an icon as "an artifact that crystallizes and embodies a set of mental associations far beyond its functionality and immediate environment." Levi's 501 jeans, of course, are one of the most iconic brands in history, a "particular vigorous set of associations of time, place and culture." I believe passion brands typically have that iconic attribute as part of their appeal.

Grasp the magic of IKEA. It's in the vision statement: from a farming village in southern Sweden to scores of countries around the world, IKEA has maintained its core values: design, function, and value. From that farming village, it has also pioneered an entire category of "first home" furniture, establishing a category that has grown to attract new entrants such as CB2, West Elm, and Pottery Barn.

Peter Connolly, retail maven and architect of the successful introduction of IKEA into this country (after a less-than-stellar beginning in the mid-1980s), says the course was chartered in the early 1990s when he and Linda Sawyer, now CEO of Deutsch Advertising, realized that the brand had come to mean cheap.

"The marketing at first was solely focused on price," he recalls. "Every store started off with a bang and then sales steadily trended down. Linda and I listened to consumers in groups tell us they didn't buy anything from IKEA, but when they showed us pictures of their homes, we saw lamps and chairs and tables we knew had come from IKEA. When we asked about it, they'd tell us it was just temporary. They were ashamed to have it in their homes. The brand had done that to itself."

Connolly and Sawyer decided to reposition the brand away

from cheap and onward to lifestyle choice. The ads moved from being about five-cent forks and nine-dollar lamps to a young couple buying a well-designed living room suite for less than fifteen hundred dollars. They showed more-mature couples relying on IKEA for weekend house furnishings.

To make the IKEA point in an exciting way, Connolly used the Elizabeth, New Jersey, store—where he started out as manager before being promoted to chief marketing officer for the entire US division—as the source of over-the-top promotions. These ranged from bringing in tons of sand and borrowing lifeguard stands from up and down the New Jersey shore—making customers crawl over the sand to get in the door and rewarding them with free sunglasses for their effort—to having couples sleep overnight in the bedding section to win a free mattress and box spring. New York City mayor Rudy Guiliani even married one couple who won a Connolly-inspired contest.

One of his seminal initiatives predated the rise of pop-up stores: he launched a ministore, termed an "outpost," on 57th and Lexington Avenue in New York City. Every three months he changed the focus. It started as a kitchenware store, then became a lighting store, then a carpet store. Everything about it changed, not just the inventory: different uniforms for the staff, different layout, different color schemes.

Through all of it, Connolly stayed focused on the core "root stock" of IKEA, while leavening its Swedish heritage with some American wit. IKEA doesn't bring us the same furniture and accessories it did a generation ago. The idea of IKEA is and has been flexible, adaptable furniture and accessories, scalable to small and large dwellings. What it has preserved is a utilitarian approach to modern home furnishings and an emphasis on cost containment that ensures IKEA's relevance on our to-do lists: from dorm room to apartment to family room to weekend getaway.

IKEA'S ENVIRONMENTAL PROGRAM

IKEA's commitment to sustainability predates the current world emphasis: IKEA began taking serious environmental measures in 1992.

1. Replace polyvinyl chloride (PVC) in wallpapers, home textiles, shower curtains, lampshades and furniture
2. Minimize the use of formaldehyde in its products, including textiles
3. Eliminate acid-curing lacquers
4. Produce a model of chair (OGLA) made from 100 percent pre-consumer waste
5. Introduce a series of air-inflatable furniture
6. Reduce the use of chromium for metal surface treatment
7. Limit the use of substances such as cadmium, lead, PCB, PCP, and AZO pigments
8. Use wood from responsibly managed forests that replant and maintain biological diversity
9. Use only recyclable materials for flat packaging and "pure" (non-mixed) materials for packaging to assist in recycling

The company's reliance on the flat pack, that amazing shipping container first designed to be used by customers taking their wares home on public transportation, is going through an expanded redefinition: the flat pack house, working to reduce the cost of home ownership for first-time buyers. Today, IKEA is definitely a long way from the founding vision of Ingvar Kamprad in 1943, who began by selling pens, wallets, picture frames, and anything else he could get on the cheap. But it is a living, breathing organism breeding tremendous brand enthusiasm among the value conscious in thirty-five countries around the world.

If a brand doesn't have roots, it can create personality with a series of successful small gestures of its own, as long as they ratchet up authentic affection. Remember GEICO. Imagine what another company might have done to create a relaunch for the moribund Government Employees Insurance Company?

There is another type of mythos, as well, to consider. The personal mythos, as in "How I Came to Love This Brand" stories. These are part and parcel of passion brand legend and lore. They are often kicked off in what researchers Harper and Michelle Roehm term flashbulb memories—a term more typically used to describe negative public events, such as the death of a public official or an extremely horrible news event. Think of the assassination of John or Robert Kennedy or the 9-11 tragedy and our ability to preserve in memory's narration every detail of our personal experience of these horrible events. Crucial elements of the flashbulb phenomenon are how "vividly detailed and resistant to forgetting and therefore enduring over time."[4] The event is so powerful that many of the details are caught up in a profoundly personal context, rather than solely in the event that caused the bulb to flash.

The Roehms, both academics albeit at different universities in North Carolina, decided to look at the same phenomenon from a marketer's perspective. They quote at the outset a twenty-five-year-old memory as told to them of a first experience with Krispy Kreme doughnuts. "I remember it like it was yesterday. I was eleven and we were visiting my cousins, who lived in the South at that time. As a special treat, my aunt and my cousin and I went to the Krispy Kreme one morning. There were some hot doughnuts that had just been made and we had them right after they were done. I remember the smell, the taste of the doughnuts. I remember my cousin making fun of me, because I ate mine so fast and I got glaze all over myself, on my face, my hands, everything." This powerful product memory includes—as do those associated with shocking news events—tremendous layers of detail, sensory information, time of day, context, and people who participated with her.

The conclusion is clear: novelty is crucial, a sense of surprise can produce the requisite flash. Naturally, first movers in categories can be said to offer such novelty cues. Build-a-Bear Workshop is another brand the Roehms found that met the criteria. But novelty is more than innovation. Novelty is personal. It may not be new to the marketplace, but if it's new to me there's the opportunity for a flashbulb moment.

I remember such a moment for me with Elizabeth Arden cosmetics. I had gone through all of four years at Indiana University wearing blue jeans and white oxford cloth shirts, long hair pulled into a pony tail, no makeup, and Adidas sneakers (I think). Pretty much it was the uniform of the serious student of the day. Then, all of a sudden I was going to graduate and go on job interviews. Things seemed ready to spool out of control pretty quickly.

For college graduation, my second cousins from Memphis sent me an Elizabeth Arden makeup kit, undoubtedly a gift-with-purchase promotion. I'd never really seen such a thing or confronted such a series of choices—foundation, lipstick, eye shadow, blush—it was, to say the least, overwhelming. And yet there was a pamphlet inside the kit that spoke directly to me with very basic and friendly "how-to" information. I remember sitting down on the bed and just reading, trying, looking in the mirror, and making the effort. I was extremely grateful, both to my Memphis cousins and to Elizabeth Arden Cosmetics, which I still rely upon. I've never seriously considered using anything else.

I believe that some brands are poised to enter our lives at key moments, those when a flashbulb really does go off. In my own work, when I team up with Hal Goldberg to hypnotize consumers, I always have him follow that same syntax of questions I outlined earlier: first, what is the most powerful and most recent memory of the category? Second, what is the most powerful and most recent memory of the specific brand for which I'm consulting?

We find that the first and most powerful memories meet the criteria of the flashbulb going off. These memories, which are more easily accessed through hypnosis, are wonderfully rich, detailed, sensory, and contextual. The most recent memories, however, are typically dull, flat, and disappointing. It's the dissonance between the promise of the brand experience—as felt in those early memories—and the letdown in the reality of today's more mundane usage that points the way to reinvigorating a brand. What we're attempting to do is get the current personal brand story back in line with the original and very compelling personal narration the consumer tells herself.

One consumer's first experience with Trix cereal was in opposition to her mother's refusal to ever purchase it, because it was "sugary fluff." The now forty-something mother was transported back to the world in which she wanted oh so very much to eat the Trix with the funny bunny rabbit she watched in the commercials: "Silly rabbit, Trix are for kids," she remembered with a laugh. And yet her mother wouldn't let her have it. It was a memory of deprivation, alleviated by a sleepover at a friend's house and the treat of Trix before heading home. Her most powerful memory? Serving Trix to her own daughter and laughing with her about how colorful and delicious it was. Her most recent? Being irritated when the box she bought seemed filled mostly with air and not very much cereal. Deprivation again.

These personal narrations are the harbingers of any brand's real equity, their profound connection woven in and through our private memories. Every brand has this to rely upon, whether or not there's a fabulous backstory to the brand itself.

Two strangely similar brands became true north on the compass for me as I started investigating the company mythos-as-marketing aspect of the passion brand phenomenon: Jack Daniel's and Camel. Both had held firmly onto their roots, albeit in distinctly different fashions. Let's start with Jack.

"We're Tennessee whiskey," Frank Bobo tells me. He's the retired head distiller who spends most of his spare time talking to people about Jack Daniel's. "We're not bourbon. We're just about the only folks that can lay a claim to that. Couple of others have come along, but we've been at it a good long time. Aged over maple charcoal we make ourselves. American oak barrels. Been that way since we started."[5]

That tone of voice is amazing, and not just because it's so spectacularly authentic coming from the retired head distiller as we walk around the Jack Daniel's distillery in Lynchburg, Tennessee. It's amazing because nearly everyone I talk to adopts the same kind of gnarled, folksy, "gosh I don't know nothing 'bout marketing ma'am, but I sure do love to talk about Jack" tone. And, of course, it's also the precise tone of Jack Daniel's advertising and its Web site. It's like talking to the brand itself.

The "marketing fellow" isn't around, but I'm given a note that he left for me. "Kate, I'm sorry I missed you this afternoon. The contractor who built this building for us called me this afternoon and asked me to go fishing with him. We've been trying to do this forever, so I'm going. I hope you got the information you're seeking. It was good meeting you. Warm regards . . ."

Is the "gone fishing" sign genuine or a ruse? Does this marketing guy really embody the brand personality that perfectly or is his note an intricate screen through which Jack Daniel's filters every communication? Another brand might well blow off a writer, but I can't think of many that would opt for this particular gambit. Whatever it is, it is charming. I'm delighted, really, to wander around on my own and to think of a corporate executive who goes fishing instead of making sure I get the story straight.

I don't think it's something they've been trained to do, but encouraged to do. The company culture planted years ago is one that Jack Daniel's and its ad agency decided not to get in the way of. One of my favorite quotes is attributed to Michelangelo when he was asked how he came to sculpt David. He is reported to have said, "I went to the quarry. I chose the marble. I took away everything that *wasn't* David." That's what a great and rooted brand like Jack Daniel's can do: Just let the brand speak for itself.

Frank Bobo, the stand-in for the marketing fellow, tells me "I figured we'd just go out and take a walk around and I'd introduce you to folks. I asked to be able to take you around, but pretty much anybody who works here knows how to do the job. We all qualify by taking the tour twelve times and then taking Joe on a tour to prove we can do it right."

How many other companies have each employee take the tour twelve times and then give it to the head of marketing? I wonder. My guess: None that boast a billion-dollar international brand.

So Frank starts me off with a bit of history: "The Old No. 7 on the label comes from a story that old Mr. Lem told me. I'm pretty sure it's the real one. Seems like Jack Daniel sent out a barrel to a distributor in Kansas and it was marked with a seven. Come to find out, it didn't get there. So, Jack sends him another one. Just by coincidence that one was marked seven also. Then, the railroad found the first barrel, so they delivered it—but marked it 'Old Number 7.' The guy wrote back asking for more of the 'Old Number 7,' cause he thought it was better. Jack just started labeling everything Old Number 7."

That ability to deal with happenstance in a totally unflappable if eccentric way appears to become part of the DNA of the brand over time. As one of the fellows I met down there told me, "We figured out that the barrels up top in the warehouse got colder in the winter and warmer in the summer. That makes the whiskey age differently, so we let it set in those barrels and didn't blend it in: That got us to single-barrel aged Jack Daniel's."

What did single-barrel aged Jack Daniel's do for them? The bartender of the Admirals Club in the Nashville airport tells me soon enough. "That single-barrel stuff is amazing. Sometimes it's great; sometimes it's pretty rough. You pay more for it, but when it's great there's nothing better."

Imagine that. Spotty performance becomes part of the legend, not a detractor from it. This is one of the reasons why I believe that passion brands have extremely forgiving consumers, just as we're more forgiving of someone we care about than we are of the stranger who owns that all-night car alarm. This story also illustrates the power of passion brands to deliver margin, of course.

One of the amazing things about Jack Daniel's is that it has grown tremendously over the years, not just the number of cases shipped, dollar volumes, and contribution to Browne-Foreman's bottom line, but its styles of distillation. One of the guys tells me, "There's green label and black label. For years, that was about it. We couldn't make it fast enough. Everyone—every state, every restaurant, every bar, every liquor store—everyone was on allocation. We'd get them what we could, but we couldn't come close to getting everyone what they wanted.

"Pretty soon we noticed that some folks might like something a bit different than just green and black label. Maybe we could trade them up a bit and reduce the allocation backlog. Charge 'em more for better. We thought, if one time over the charcoal was good, what would two times do? That's where Gentleman Jack came from. Country cocktails, like Downhome Punch, Black Jack Cola, and Lynchburg Lemonade came out when folks seemed to like coolers and all. We just thought they'd like 'em with Jack Daniel's, too. Then, we noticed that visitors to Lynchburg, which is a dry county, seemed to get frustrated that they couldn't buy Jack Daniel's, so we got a bill through the legislature saying we could sell special commemorative editions in our gift shop, so we started doing that. I think I've got some of our new steak grilling sauce here, someplace, too." And on and on it goes. Absolutely on the same page, singing from the same hymnal, in perfect harmony.

Beyond the distillery, the lifeblood of the brand runs through several important arteries: There's the Lynchburg Hardware and General Store, in real space and in the virtual world. "Walk on down," they tell me, and so off I go on a dusty road, there's no better word for it than "ambling," across a creek bed, through a residential area of town where I think I may see Barney Fife strolling along on his way to have lunch with Sheriff Andy and Aunt Bee. But no, I'm just hoping to find a worn path to Main Street.

I'm going through a time warp to inspect a glittery array of merchandise, ranging from chrome bar stools with the Jack Daniel's logo embossed on the leather seats ($109) to a three-piece shot glass set with pewter emblems ($33.50), a bristle dart board ($65.50), a barrel wood bar stool ($230), and a pool table (don't ask). The passion Jack drinkers (and they do call it by its first name) feel for the brand goes well beyond the drink. They want to bond themselves to the brand and the brand to themselves, their homes, and their leisure pursuits.

There's also the fabled Tennessee Squire Association. "Here in the Hollow, we move a bit slower than the rest of the world, but we want to keep in touch with our friends. We know that some of you use electronic mail, so if you'd like for us to have your e-mail address, please fill out the card below and send it back to us. We don't want you to miss out on any news from Lynchburg." So I ask to become a squire and am "accepted." Thus begins a really remarkable aspect of the Jack Daniel's relationship. Every so often, but never in a way that I can predict, I receive various things from "the Hollow." Notices of taxes, a calendar, an update that someone's cow has started walking across my property. All messages in the distinct voice of the brand, nothing trying to sell me anything more than the very real uniqueness of Jack Daniel's. Some arrive in the mailbox in a large white envelope with a Lynchburg return address; some slip into my e-mail. In either case, they are welcomed and enjoyed. It's particularly striking when I think about how many other mailings from brands, companies, and retailers I smile to receive. That would be none.

"Lynchburg, Tennessee," one calendar explains, "is a quiet little town of white frame houses and perfect green sod . . . a place where kids go fishing, doctors make house calls, and local stores are owned by local folks. I should know. I was born and raised here in Lynchburg. And work here still as the proprietress of Miss Mary Bobo's Boarding House over at the south end of town."

Full disclosure: I can't drink Jack Daniel's. Surely I want to, but it's just not for me. That said, I have friends who will drink nothing but Jack Daniel's. Nothing else. It's reported to be the mainstay of bars throughout the world. I settle with badging my affection for the brand, if not the product, but I am in awe of how the profound specificity of the brand, with its laserlike focus on its roots, voice, and ever-expanding series of products appeals to a global audience. At first blush, it seems like it might be daunting to those without an appreciation of the shall we say, uniqueness of the South, of Tennessee, of "the Hollow." But international sales of the brand, coupled with the superpremium Gentleman Jack and Jack Daniel's & Cola, continue to drive Jack Daniel's into strong double-digit growth, boosting volume, margin, earnings, and profits, month after month, quarter after quarter.

The profound specificity of the charms of Jack somehow don't alienate. They fascinate. Even those of us who don't relish the flavor or the kick of it can appreciate the world the brand inhabits, and even want to visit its rustic birthplace on occasion.

Using a different approach, Camel cigarettes nonetheless quietly pulls forward the vital roots of the brand from its 1913 origins into twenty-first-century relevance. Camel's story is genuinely remarkable when we consider that cigarettes are viewed as a controlled substance, not allowed many of the communication tools available to virtually every other legal product: no television or no radio ads since 1971 in the United States, plus extremely limited print, age-restricted Web space, no outdoor billboard space, limited direct mail—the list goes on and on.

Still, when we conducted the passion brand survey, Camel—with its brand share that hovers in the single digits—is in a virtual tie with Marlboro, the six-hundred-pound gorilla of the American tobacco market.

"The bottom line when you look at the Camel brand, its identity is less mainstream than the other brands," explains Cressida Lozano, vice president in charge of the Camel Brand at RJ Reynolds Tobacco Company, based in Winston-Salem, North Carolina. We're having a discussion about the remarkable affection that smokers feel for Camel.[6]

"We have a 'lust for living' attitude that is more irreverent, more original. From the very beginning, that's how the brand has behaved. We're the original so our core consumers are passionate about us, because they embrace that value. It's an element of their personality. Camel does not try to be something for everyone. Everyone seems to be smoking Marlboro—we're outside that."

One of her colleagues, Richard Wise from Agent 16, Camel's longtime agency, tells me, "Camel has a much more powerful social currency. But it does not enjoy the benefit of popularity. It's a distinctive statement, which I quite understand. I find the experience of living in a mass society very unsettling, because everything blurs together. Whether it's an Albertson's in Omaha or Whole Foods in Union Square, everyone has followed the same convention: packaging, layout, aisles, carts, everything. Camel has refused to yield to the spirit of the age."[7]

"The thing specifically about Camel," Mark Morrissey, also a tenured Camel agency executive and chief executive officer of Agent 16, explained, "is that its values have been stable for a very long time: irreverence, authenticity. The longer the values are stable, the more of a 'lighthouse' it becomes: Our smokers are into self-definition and they want to show that to others."[8]

Indeed, Camel was the first mass-marketed cigarette, arriving on the scene in 1913. That arrival was a sensation, orchestrated by none other than R. J. Reynolds himself. Ads announced, "Camel is coming." But no one quite knew what to expect. Then actual camels arrived, walking down the main streets of various cities and towns around America. Then came the cigarettes, twenty to a pack, bundled and packaged for remarkable convenience versus the then-ubiquitous custom of rolling your own.

From the beginning what Camel wants to tell you about itself is there on the label: a blend of Turkish and domestic tobaccos. It seemed exotic then and it seems exotic now. "A pack of Camels is the most exotic thing you can still purchase at the corner store," Wise says, recalling what a smoker had told him in a research session.

Just as in the case of Jack Daniel's "one size doesn't fit all" aura, Camel, too, gives multiple entry points into the brand. Does the world need a new version of Camel? The Camel marketing folks view the launch of a new varietal as sitting on the pivot point between what the brand *says* about the smoker and what it *does* for the smoker. As Morrissey puts it, "A line extension reinforces an identity; it becomes a way to communicate that identity. It opens a new door to the smoker who may like the Camel heritage and image, but hasn't liked the taste up until now. With a new version, a new taste, we give them a reason to give us another try."

He contrasts this with the efforts of other megabrands like Coke, Pepsi, and Oreo to use one über-mark to bundle a series of emerging benefits, in response to smaller competitors in the market. This technique, which we see over and over again, has the impact of eroding the brand's iconic meaning as an identity badge for consumers. It gains the brand breadth but loses the depth that marks a passionate attachment.

"It feels desperate," Wise continues the thought. "We all know people pleasers who are wild for approval: Do you like me now? How about now? as they shape-shift to meet what they believe people want from them. A brand like Camel just cannot do that. A brand becomes sad, in some cases dizzying to the consumer, when it loses its way. I feel that way about Coke right now. What does it stand for?"

The economics at issue are tough for big brands, by definition. How they are to grow in response to changes in the marketplace without losing their way becomes the question for the stewards of the brand. "Megabrands like Budweiser that are trying to aggregate large share and contribute growth run-up against this all the time," says Morrissey. "They need to get more people under the umbrella. And then they need to get more people. And then more people. The larger the brand, the more desperate it is to grow, the more powerful the inertia is to shrink. It becomes extremely tricky to keep developing these huge brands that are made up of lots of little sub-brands—I actually think of it as trying to keep lots of plates spinning, like a circus act. Here's Coke! No wait, here's Diet Coke! No wait, here's Coke Zero! All the while, upstart and challenger brands seek to shift the balance."

One of the reasons über-brands use this umbrella strategy, of course, is simply the high cost of launching a new brand. When a mark, such as Coke or Budweiser, is so well known and loved, it is undeniably cheaper for marketers to extend rather than invent an entirely new mark, which then has to earn bottler enthusiasm, retail shelf space, and consumer awareness. So into our world arrives New Coke, Diet Coke, Diet Coke Plus, Coca-Cola C2, Coca-Cola Zero, Coca-Cola Cherry Zero, Coca-Cola Cherry, Diet Coke Cherry, Coca-Cola with Lemon, Diet Coke with Lemon, Coca-Cola Vanilla Zero, Coca-Cola Vanilla, Diet Coca-Cola Vanilla, Coca-Cola with Lime, Diet Coke with Lime, Coca-Cola Raspberry, Diet Coke Raspberry, Coca-Cola Black Cherry Vanilla, Diet Coke Cherry Vanilla, Coca-Cola BlāK, Diet Coca-Cola with Citrus, Coca-Cola with Orange, and Passover Coca-Cola, with pure cane sugar instead of corn syrup.

Obviously, many of these versions simply offer an added ingredient to spice things up a bit: cherry, lemon, vanilla, lime, raspberry, black cherry, or orange. Sure, it's easy enough to understand. More problematic is the competing claims among

Diet Coke, Coke Zero, and Diet Coke Plus. Does the brand have the latitude, the brand width, the consumer permission to go in so many directions? Diet Coke Plus is fortified with vitamins and minerals! It's an open question, but one rightly asked. Is Coke still the "real thing," or is it morphing into "anything"?

Then there's Bud, Bud Light, Budweiser Select, Bud Ice, Bud Ice Light, Budweiser Brew Masters Private Reserve, Bud Dry, Bud Silver, Bud Extra, Budweiser/Bud Light Chelada (with Clamato Juice!), and now Bud Light Lime, looking a lot like a response to Mexican brand Corona. The big guys seemingly have to compete head to head with smaller, more facile brands, while not estranging their core audiences or losing their identity. It's a hard line to walk for megabrands, but they are assisted, of course, by the raw muscle of brand share (how much of the market they command), category captaincy in retail venues (how many stores, taverns, and eateries they are in), marketing clout, and efficiencies of scale.

A study of brand extensions in the *Journal of Marketing Research* in 1999 does provide solace to the Oreos of the world, a brand extended with Cakesters, Double Stuff, Golden Originals, Pure White Fudge Covered, and Winter with Red Crème—and its Mini-Bite Size Snak Saks, Mini-Bite Size Go-Pak, and Mini-Bite Size nine-ounce bags.

According to the researchers, "Fortunately for brand managers, the research reported here suggests that retrieval (memory) processes such as categorization, recognition, and recall are also fairly immune to the potentially diluting effects of extensions. . . . Established brands are shown here to benefit from the introduction of extension, but there are costs involved in shifting promotional funds from a parent brand to an extension. Although exposure to brand extension advertising facilitated recall of parent brands, the facilitative effect was not as great as that resulting from exposure to parent brand advertising."[9]

Minor, newsworthy trademarks (Oreo Double Stuff) within the larger franchise (Oreo) may help a big brand look smaller and more select, off-setting the peril of "same old, same old, different day" ubiquity, while gaining stature from the big brand imprimatur. It may well be important to create newsworthy extensions and it certainly is more cost effective than trying to create a new brand from the ground up. But marketers should not walk away from reminding consumers of the power and joy of the original Oreo, Crest, or Coke. The temptation is to advertise only the newsworthy new entrants rather than continue to invest in plain old Coke, but it's a temptation to be avoided since it's the original version that provides the permission to believe in the small newcomer.

But what of smaller brands? What of Camel, which currently has twenty-seven versions available. Too much? Too confusing? The research study, in fact, says that "nondominant brands" actually benefit more from product extensions than big brands. As Wise pointed out, a Camel is a distinct experience, but not a universally popular one. Thus, twenty-seven varieties of Camels provide multiple doorways into the brand, making it more accessible while ensuring that it stays relevant and on the smoker's radar. The popularity competition may be won by Marlboro, but not the *personality* competition. Ditto Coke versus Red Bull. Ditto for any spirit versus Jack Daniel's. Ditto Starbucks versus Peet's.

Wise poses a question: What other brand has ever inspired a piece of modern literary fiction that takes place entirely inside its package? Sure enough, the book *Still Life with Woodpecker* by Tom Robbins (1981) has a pack of Camels on its cover, actually *as* its cover, if you don't mind that the camel in question is a woodpecker. The dialogue includes such "postmodern-day fairy tale" insights as "There are two kinds of people in this world: those who believe there are two kinds of people in this world and those who are smart enough to know better." The ability of the Camel-esque pack to telegraph meaning is underscored by the use of the book by the Lucy Whitmore (Drew Barrymore) character in the film *50 First Dates*.

The point Wise is making is one that illustrates how passion brands operate in our consumer culture: they do help us tell ourselves and others a bit about ourselves. Passion brands are used in television, film, and art to help the audience understand something about a character. A character smokes a Camel, asks for a Tanqueray gin martini "shaken not stirred," or orders a Cosmopolitan with her girlfriends, and we know something more about these characters.

If further proof were required, Wise has a second question: You're sitting in a café. There's an artist sitting next to you and he's doodling on a napkin with a pack of cigarettes at the ready. What brand is it? "Camel, of course," he says. "There's something in the brand that cries out, 'Step into this. Make it your own.'" That invitation to participate, to tell yourself and others about you through the brand, is the call to passionate attachment. It can't come from "outer space," just as a stranger calling to us to come "join the fun" isn't anywhere nearly as compelling as a long-term friend, someone whose roots we know and to a degree share, or want to.

Passion branding is great, of course, when it works, but what happens to a one-time passion brand when it doesn't stick to its roots? This is a cautionary tale. I turned to Daryl Brewster, again, this time not as the former head of Nabisco but in his next role as president and CEO of Krispy Kreme, a spot he held from 2006 to 2008, taking the fabled brand from an on-the-ropes, punchdrunk has-been to being a contender.

The essential "secret" of a Krispy Kreme doughnut is to eat

it hot. It's formed from dough extruded by air pressure to form a perfect doughnut shape. Technically, there isn't such a thing as a doughnut "hole" at Krispy Kreme. It's light and airy—and the joy of eating one hot is hard to overestimate. Scores of people tell me that it's possible to get the next best thing by microwaving a Krispy Kreme for one second, perhaps two. Opinions vary.

How could something so simple and delicious go wrong? Brewster's understanding of the past economic foibles of the brand is anchored to the old real estate edict: location, location, location.

"The roots of Krispy Kreme were Southern roots," Brewster explained to me in an interview over lunch. "We started in Winston-Salem and the model was fabulous: a manufacturing facility, a bakery, on the periphery of a town in cheap, industrial space, making terrific doughnuts that they'd load up on trucks and take to local grocery and convenience stores. At its heart, it wasn't a walk-up business: The basic proposition was bake it and take it. They just stumbled on the walk-up business, people driving miles out of their way if they thought that they could get them fresh—so they started using a 'hot light' to signal that a batch was coming out."[10]

Then came the franchises. What happened in the '70s, '80s and '90s to Krispy Kreme was an overabundance of optimism in the franchise model, and a misunderstanding of the brand's "bake it and take it" real estate roots. This was not a fast-food business; it was a bakery that delivered to local stores. That got lost in the heat of the moment.

First, in 1976 it was acquired by Beatrice Foods, which had little insight as to what to do with a doughnut company but thought it would be fun to have one. When that paled by 1982, a group of franchisees purchased it back from Beatrice. Unfortunately, in that go-go franchise era, Krispy Kreme was modeled after Dunkin' Donuts. Having one on every street corner might have been a good idea for Dunkin', but not for Krispy Kreme, whose success had been as a bakery, not a quick-serve restaurant.

According to Brewster's explanation to me during our interview, "You need a lot of pretty expensive retail real estate to execute that approach and for much of the '80s and '90s the company tried to be a manufacturing site in a retail setting. So you needed five- thousand-square-foot spaces to make the doughnuts in a location where people can wander in for breakfast. The Krispy Kreme business had always been a dozens business. People buy them and take them to work. It wasn't a place to hang out and have a doughnut and a cup of coffee. You don't mind driving out of your way to buy a couple of dozen doughnuts, so in the brand's heyday, we would get stories of drivers crossing two lanes of heavy traffic on the highway if they saw the hot light was on."

The economics of the successful Krispy Kreme model got buried under neophytes who swarmed to it, hoping to make a "killing" in a fast-food franchise. Stores opened with huge hoopla. There were news articles, television coverage, people standing in line around the block. You have to sell a lot of doughnuts to pay for retail space with the square footage to run the all-important bakery lines. If you don't make it in the morning rush, you're not going to make it.

Nonetheless, expansion outside of the Southern heritage of the brand continued at a breakneck pace, eventually reaching forty-five states, as well as the District of Columbia and moving into Mexico, Australia, Canada, and England. According to Brewster, the move into new areas was complicated by the lack of roots for the brand.

"People in the South grew up with Krispy Kreme and for them, it really is a 'no substitute will do' brand," he explains.

"The move outside that natural and passionate constituency was at once newsworthy and exciting, but also debatable. In the Northeast, you'd get real debates about the relative merits of Krispy Kreme versus Dunkin' Donuts. That is unthinkable in the South. In the South, there may be alternatives, but there is no substitute."

There's a great deal of life in the Krispy Kreme brand, of course. Every day the chain makes 7.5 million doughnuts—that's 2.7 billion doughnuts a year roughly—so they are doing many things right. They've figured out how to reduce the retail "footprint" so that rent can be better managed as a cost of doing business. They've retrenched from areas where the franchise system hasn't worked. They've created some new versions, including whole-grain doughnuts. Their entire product line has gone trans-fat free.

From Brewster's perspective, Krispy Kreme is poised to begin an ascent again: "The reception of the brand internationally is actually much more the way Krispy Kreme is viewed in the South, which is tremendous for it. Once more, it's in the space where people say, 'There may be alternatives, but no substitute,' and that's where it competes to win."

The potential for Krispy Kreme to recapture its glory days, albeit in new ways and new markets, shows the resilience of a once and future passion brand. An article in the *New York Times Magazine* by Rob Walker poses this question: "Can a dead brand live again?" He writes of many of the great brands that have disappeared, not because consumers didn't love them, but because the multinational corporations that acquired them didn't view them as having the legs to straddle the globe.[11]

"If commerce is part of the American fabric, then brands are part of the American fabric," Paul Earle, president of RiverWest, told Walker. "When a brand goes away, a piece of

Americana goes away." RiverWest is a firm that focuses on buying brands on the decline. Among those already in its portfolio are Nuprin, Brim (remember "fill it to the rim?"), Salon Selectives, and Eagle Snacks.

Can it be done? Think of Converse. "Ours is retro fashion," says Mike Shine, the creative director at Converse's ad agency. "Jackson Pollack, Kurt Cobain, Joey Ramone: these are the last people in the world who would ever want to see a commercial for Chuck Taylors. We're a ninety-seven-year-old brand with a deep allegiance to the Chuck Taylor culture."[12]

"Deep allegiance" is an excellent turn of phrase to explain the authenticity that Converse enthusiasts attribute to the brand. It stands for some things like creativity, nonconformity, and iconoclasm, values that don't lend themselves to commercial mass marketing. The Gap may try to bring back khakis by reminding us that "Gene Kelly wore Khakis," but somehow it doesn't work. It diminishes both the Gap and Gene Kelly as we find ourselves wondering, Who said it was okay to use his image to sell pants?

This deep allegiance is not a nostalgia play. You don't bring it back to have it the way it was or to hearken back to simpler times. According to Stephen Brown, "Retromarketing is not merely a matter of reviving dormant brands and foisting them on softhearted, dewy-eyed, nostalgia-stricken consumers. It involves working with consumers to co-create an oasis of authenticity for tired and thirsty travelers through the desert of mass-produced marketing dreck."[13]

One of the ways to gain a deep allegiance is suggested by the way many brands naturally gravitate to an iconic person to embody its personality and benefits. Thus, Kurt Cobain, Joey Ramone, Jackson Pollack. In other cases, the brand's genesis story creates a cult of personality: Steve Jobs, Robert Mondavi, Jack Daniel.

Indeed, a fabulous article from *Networking Knowledge* suggests that Steve Jobs has become a "human logo," so inextricably entwined is his name with the technology and technological design enhancements of our time. Writer Chloe Peacock of the University of Brighton in Britain looks at Jobs as the exemplar of what she terms this time of "late modernity," when people have been able to brand themselves.[14]

The process is one of "metonym," through which a part is meant to suggest much more than the whole. She uses as an example Margaret Thatcher, the former prime minister of England whose name has come to mean a time of privatization, monetarism, and nationalism. Princess Diana similarly suggests a time of intense national grieving or even hysterics. Steve Jobs in this sense stands for all that is real about the oftentimes depersonalizing world of technology.

Few genesis stories are as literally appropriated as the one she quotes from *The Cult of Mac*: "In the beginning (of the Information Age) was the void. And the void was digital. But lo there came upon the land, the shadow of Steve Jobs (and Stephen Wozniak) and Steven (Stephen) said, 'Let there be Apple,' and there was Apple. And Steven (Stephen) beheld Apple. And it was good."[15]

Jobs's backstory is a classic ennobling quest: a small-college dropout becomes a high-tech "phreak," in the parlance of the 1970s, lives hand to mouth as an entrepreneur working from his parent's garage, but later emerges as founder and chief stockholder of a $2 billion company, only to be displaced and disgraced as its chief executive officer in exile, then becomes a resurrected titan of technology and a prostate cancer survivor. Jobs's story in many ways encapsulates not just Apple's story but a human struggle as well.

His black turtleneck and jeans attire is comfortably familiar and approachable yet striking in its departure from classic CEO garb. Yet he is CEO of one of the most successful companies in the history of capitalism. By making Apple accessible—through his sheer humanity—we find the brand more appealing.

"Jobs mediates attitudes and beliefs on fate, spirituality, love and counterculture which, one could argue, contradict the values of a corporation such as Apple within a capitalist system," Peacock writes. "But since he is able to resolve the conflict between competing philosophies on a level of personal experience, it transforms into a resolution for the brand identity as well." It's in the resolution of this tension between Apple's counterculture roots and its current size and scale that makes the narrative of Jobs's life and the force of his personality such a powerful interface between product and consumer.

The consumer then becomes a willing participant in the mythlike creation of the Apple brand, as we take in news, information, and images about Jobs and apply them to what is, after all, a corporate entity. The marketing machinery of advertising, public relations, and promotion moves away from product news and information, away from the mercantile benefits of the marketplace—growing and expanding a business—and onto a very different plain of consumer/brand conspiracy, if you will: a collusion to embrace a sincere, authentic philosophy via a brand.

Emblematic of the approachability of the brand is the tremendous variety in the ways enthusiasts can stake out a piece of Apple for their own: Macintosh User Groups (MUGs) abound. There's IMUG, for international users group, multilingual users, and designers; CMUG, for Christian Macintosh computing, providing theological connections as well as the typical tech support; I/O MUG, an Internet-only users group that wants to improve the system by sharing information, support, and ideas for Mac users throughout the cybersphere; and

NHMUG, for NASA employees, helping them stay current with Mac technology developments and how best to apply them.

That notion of cocreation is how these passion brands achieve their remarkable vitality and stay buzzworthy, the topic to which we will next turn.

WHAT WE TALK ABOUT WHEN WE TALK ABOUT BRANDS

Mine the Mythos

Verbatim Consumer Quotes

"Man, I know all about Jobs. He was just a dork and then got Apple started and then got booted out and started Pixar and Next and a whole bunch of other stuff. Then they brought him back to Apple 'cause they couldn't really do it without him. He's the real deal. You can tell it just by looking at him. I mean he hasn't sold out, he's not some corporate tycoon kind of guy, he's in it for the money, sure, but also because he's really still a dork at heart."

"Belvedere was started by Ann Lander's nephew or Dear Abby's son, or some such. I think he just went over to Poland after the fall of the Iron Curtain and convinced people to make vodka for him. Then he got a great bottle and started advertising in the *Wall Street Journal*. That's where I saw it first. Same upper corner of the paper every day. Really expensive. Something like made out of Polish rye or something? It just seemed so clean and then too it was more expensive, so it must be better. So I started drinking it. My guy at the liquor store told me about it, I think. I just liked the clean taste, better distilled or more often or something like that? I heard Skye vodka keeps you from having hangovers, but I've stuck with Belvedere all the same."

"There's this guy down the street and he hand rolls cigars right there in the window. Same stuff as Cohiba's from Cuba, but not illegal. He makes them right there. His family came from Cuba and they took the seeds from the tobacco plants with them when they left in the '60s and planted them somewhere else in South America, but it's the same plants as Cuba. That's how he gets the tobacco and he rolls the cigars right there while you watch. It's really something to see, like he's not even looking at them as he makes them. But they come out perfectly."

"I went on a winery tour on Long Island, Hargrave and then Bidwell. You know they have a great climate out there for growing a certain kind of grape. Just the right kind of soil and growing season. Kind of amazing really. They used to use the land only for growing potatoes! But now, it's really gorgeous and we drank some really terrific wines. Sat on this deck overlooking the vineyard at dusk and just enjoyed ourselves. I think they charged a couple of bucks, but it was a good deal. Hard to get, but every once in a while you see them on a good restaurant's list. I bought a couple of cases and everybody likes them. We even did a tasting for friends when we came back; I got those kind of wafers to 'clear our palate,' ahem! but it was fun. Our friends really liked it. We like to go see local things when we travel like that. We've seen wineries and cheese makers in North Carolina and had some pretty terrific local wines in Wisconsin. It's fun. You get to really meet local people and understand why they do what they do. We love doing it."

Chapter 8
BRAND THE BUZZ

This is a true story, guaranteed by a good friend who swears to its accuracy.

There used to be a Krispy Kreme store on West 23rd Street in New York. The fellow in question—let's call him Mark—lived on 14th Street and had worked out a signal with a friend—Sam—who lived across the street from Krispy Kreme. When the "hot light" was on, Sam would call Mark to alert him and Mark would jog nine blocks to the store and buy a dozen donuts. He would then stroll gleefully down Broadway, joyously munching them on the way home, having "earned" the right to indulge by jogging. One day on the way home, he was feeling perhaps a bit guilty, or at least full, and saw a homeless man on the street. Mark asked the guy if he'd like to have a Krispy Kreme or two. The fellow replied, "Are they hot?"

A story about a brand like this is delicious in many respects. It's just a great story, it keeps you engaged, and it has as its punch line the brand benefit. It cries out to be told and retold, because it's *almost* as much fun as eating a warm Krispy Kreme

BRANDING PROCESS STEP 7

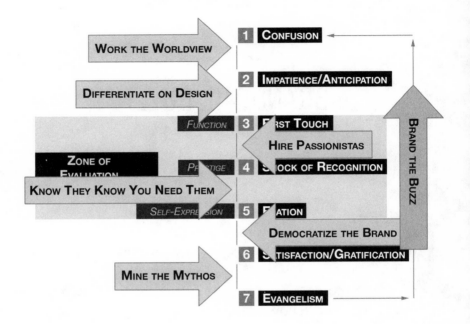

and nowhere near the calories of eating a dozen, even after a nine-block jog. There are certain brands, and certainly Krispy Kreme is one of them, in which consumers simply delight.

As Daryl Brewster told me, "It's not just consumers who love some brands; sometimes the media just seems to, too. And that's a tremendous asset, but I'm not sure how you can predict it or create it. It just seems natural, but when it happens you can feel the wind at your back. When we launched a heart-shaped Krispy Kreme for Valentine's Day, the media literally just 'ate it up.' More than 150 million impressions, national television like the *Today Show* and all the way down to small local weeklies. Same thing with the whole-grain donut. People just love to say—and write—great things about this brand."[1]

A case in point of a brand that was written is Amazon. As Joe Nocera, the Talking Business columnist of the *New York*

Times, writes, Amazon is worth an entire column just because it did one good deed for him, at Christmas.[2] It seems Nocera had ordered a PlayStation for one of his sons. It had been delivered and signed for by a neighbor, who then left it in the hallway. The PlayStation was stolen, less than a week before Christmas. Nocera called Amazon knowing that he "didn't have a leg to stand on." But Amazon replaced it in time for Christmas and didn't even charge for shipping.

It was a happy ending for Nocera and his son, yes indeed. But it caused him to take a look at Amazon's business model and come away amazed and impressed. He writes about the Charlie Rose talk show interview in which Jeff Bezos, Amazon's founder and chief executive officer, waxes lyrical about the need to be "obsessed" with the customer experience. That obsession pays off with high sales, consistent profit, and amazing consumer loyalty. As Nocera puts it, "Why would I ever shop anywhere else online?" And, as he quotes Suresh Kotha, a management professor at the University of Washington Business School, "Jeff used to say that if you did something good for one customer, they would tell a hundred customers." Nocera surely did, and so am I.

Amazon increasingly gives people things to talk about in addition to spectacular customer service, although that's quite a lot. The introduction of its Kindle ebook display device is an adroit illustration of how a massive retailer can be a game changer for several industries.

A couple of weeks ago, Mattie and I were visiting our friends Serra Yavuz and Joe Sahid, and their daughter, Olivia. Serra had just purchased her Kindle and was extolling the virtues. I had, of course, heard about it from news reports, but this had become a passion brand for Serra. She became the extended personal sales force for the Kindle brand, and by extension, Amazon.

Kindle is a wireless reading device. It mimics the look of paper with its sharp, high-resolution screen. There are no cables, no computer, and no synching. Wireless connectivity (paid for by Amazon with no additional charge to the Kindle owner) enables the immediate gratification of shopping at the Kindle store for one of 130,000 books—any one of which can be downloaded in less than a minute, and most for $9.99 or less. US and foreign newspapers and magazines are also wirelessly delivered automatically, along with sample first chapters of any book you're thinking about ordering.

All of this I knew. What I hadn't experienced was the touch and feel of the thing, roughly the size of a paperback, but weighing in at only 10.3 ounces. This was the power of Serra's evangelism. She put the thing in my hand and had me fiddle with it, all the while extolling the rationale for her decision to buy: "Just think about it for traveling." Serra, Joe, and Olivia often take off for a month or so on an extended trip in the summer. Her joy in the idea of having more than two hundred titles, plus newspapers stored on the device and available at her fingertips was palpable.

The price of $399 might at first seem high, but when compared to the schlep factor of totting books for herself, Joe, and Olivia, searching for newspapers and magazines in airport newsstands, and disposing of books once read in order to free up more suitcase space for fresh acquisitions only augmented the basic appeal. Pretty much any book—98 of the 112 current books on the *New York Times* best sellers list—is at hand.

Serra walked me through the elation of ownership: the "paperlike" vertical screen, the "Whispernet" technology connected via Sprint to get stuff fast, the lightness, the ergonomic design, the long battery life. It was like she'd just graduated from a sales training course, but this is of course typical of the muscle of brand buzz. As Stephen Brown told me about a colleague who'd just converted to Apple from a PC, "He seems to spend all his time bringing the brand up to the rest of us. I reckon he's on a percentage or a retainer of some kind."[3] He's not, of course. He's getting a compensation of an entirely different sort.

It's that tremor of excitement and pride in talking about a beloved brand that catalyzes word of mouth into buzz: it's the passion. As Brewster pointed out, it's extremely hard to predict or create. The art of generating buzz, some say, began in the 1980s with Absolut Vodka. Absolut developed a persuasive and scalable tool to launch discussion rather than wait and hope for it to spark spontaneously. How did they manage to generate word of mouth, which is usually just the happy by-product of a brand that performs well functionally?

The Absolut story, as told to me by Richard Lewis, its guiding star, is a fabulous example of the integration of product, position, price, packaging, promotion, and providence, the "six P's." It was the company's decision to market a vodka from Sweden in a clear apothecary bottle without a conventional label at a premium price, but it was Lewis's vision to create a now-legendary series of witty ads that focused almost unilaterally on the name. The format calls for a two-word headline (one word always being Absolut) and a full-frontal shot of the bottle, sometimes dressed by fashion designers or otherwise inspired and aspiring artists.

He and US importer Michel Roux also believed in giving away the product at cause-related events and in appropriate places. According to *Business Week*, Roux, at first the lone salesman for the brand, "leavened raw commercialism with considerable idealism. He was deeply involved in numerous charitable organizations and was one of the first marketers to unabashedly court gay consumers in an era when that was still considered risky."[4]

In hindsight, these decisions seem obvious; we know Absolut became the best-selling vodka in the world. But at the time it wasn't so apparent. In the early years, Roux bartered ties and scarves to earn flight attendants' willingness to give out Absolut miniatures in first class. He convinced Andy Warhol to do a rendering of the bottle for an ad, even though Warhol was a teetotaler. Warhol reportedly started using Absolut as cologne; he certainly paved the way for Absolut art, along with Keith Haring, Damien Hirst, and Jean-Michel Basquiat. Soon, fashion designers signed on, including John Galliano, Gianni Versace, and Tom Ford.

It's crucial to point out that Absolut did not find "brand-name artists" to create a halo for its products. Roux was best described as "daring" in his choices. "The Absolut thing completely changed my life," artist Rod English told *Business Week*. "Before that, I had spent five years living in dire poverty on Avenue D in Manhattan. I couldn't even get galleries to look at slides of my work."[5] Afterward, galleries throughout the United States and Japan welcomed him.

As Lewis explained to me in an interview, "The decision to use the word Absolut in absolutely every headline—and the bottle starring in every ad—would have been anathema to guys like me, but we saw the charm in it, its remarkable resonance. Then it became fabulous and fashionable and fun and really opened the brand up to engagement with bartenders and consumers. Everyone else was selling; we were winking, just like a great moment at a cocktail lounge."[6]

He should know. The reason he wrote the book about Absolut is that he literally wrote the Absolut story in real time, ad by ad, Christmas card insert by Christmas card cum Absolute ad insert. Lewis created more than an advertising campaign. He created a "destination." People looked forward to arriving at Absolut in the pages of their magazines and then to talking about it with friends while sending those cards to family.

One of the saddest facets of marketing is that the more a

brand performs the way you expect it to perform, the less interesting it becomes. This is an especially troubling fact of life for vodka, a clear liquid with little taste and less smell. There are just two ways around this law of diminishing interest, and they illustrate how and why buzz must become an integral part of a passion brand's business plan and how Absolut achieved buzz perfection in the Roux-Lewis years.

This model shows the problem at a glance: Everybody is using all the typical tactics to vault over the "Indifference Zone": new products, new packaging, new promotions, new channels. But only a fraction of that information ever gets through to the place where we actually integrate the information. A smaller

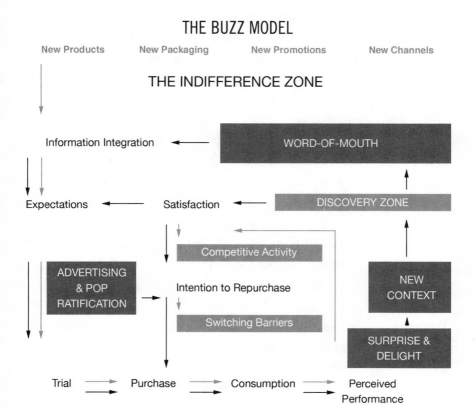

THE BUZZ MODEL

number of consumers processes the information and develops expectations. Then an ever tinier group is moved to try, purchase, consume, and evaluate the brand's performance.

Even if the brand performs to our satisfaction, we will encounter competitive activities, plus our own forgetfulness. These further reduce our intention to repurchase. Slowly, inexorably, over time, fewer and fewer of us will buy that good old trusted product. It has lost its luster.

Notice how without Surprise and Delight and New Contexts a brand quickly becomes usual. There's nothing to talk about; the brand has lost its excitement since everyone has the same expectations and experience. A brand that simply satisfies its consumer becomes vulnerable to competitors offering discounts, rebates, and other price promotions, all of which subvert the intention to repurchase the brand product, eroding consumer loyalty before it has even had the chance to start.

Brands can fight back: (1) commit to *surprise and delight* your consumers as an essential principle of business; and (2) *show up* in new and exciting contexts. This is Absolut marketing history in a box.

Absolut illustrates the effectiveness of this antidote to brand rigor mortis: in everything it does, from the look of its bottle to the way it markets, to the innovative event strategy it created to the introduction of new flavors, the brand consistently seeks to surprise and delight.

We can see the craft borrowed from Absolut in the launch of the Mini Cooper. It used no traditional media. The cars seemed to show up randomly at high-profile events. Piggybacked on SUVs, the Mini Coopers were hauled around major American cities to make the size and economy message in a compelling "You'll never guess what I saw!" way that sparked spontaneous combustion.

There was a Web site: "The SUV Backlash Starts Here."

THE PITFALL OF BEING A "ONE TRICK PONY"

Several years ago, Salem cigarettes noticed that menthol smokers had a curious habit with a new pack of cigarettes: They'd take the first cigarette out of the pack, turn it around and replace it in the pack, filter down. This cigarette, the brand learned, was the one that they would not give to someone asking to "bum" a cigarette.

The brand thought this piece of smoker behavior could be powerful to acknowledge: It started making one cigarette in each pack with a green filter. Menthol smokers immediately "got it." They knew this was the one meant to go filter down back in the pack—and they loved it. Salem was signaling that it understood. Menthol smokers started talking about the green filter, surprised and delighted by the gesture.

But, what do you do next?

There's no point in making a red filter next week.

This illustrates the pitfall of not thinking all the way through a surprise and delight strategy: A brand must have a reservoir of tactics, a continuous stream of gestures that will make the brand experience exciting and worth talking about.

There was the *Playboy* centerfold: "Weight: 2,678 pounds. Turn-ons: Hairpins, S-bends."

There were the stunts. Passing one down through the grandstands at major sports events; enthusiasts cheering the arrival of delivery flatbeds and camping outside showrooms to get a crack at a test drive.

There were the cryptic billboards. Two-tone color scheme and a one-word slogan: Motoring.

There was the perception of scarcity: A strictly limited number of authorized dealers, only fifty-six initially.

There were those sales: The allocation of Mini Coopers for the United States sold out in three months.

But being about buzz isn't just being about well-orchestrated prompts to get people to notice a brand. Sometimes it means courting controversy. Basquiat, after all, died of a drug overdose. Fashion designer Gianni Versace was murdered. Ronald Feldman, a lower Manhattan art dealer, told *Business Week*, "Absolut wasn't afraid of controversy. They knew if they could get trendsetters to drink Absolut, other people would follow."[7]

Some of the best examples of the buzz factor are also the most obvious. Consider Virgin Atlantic, in fact, the entire Virgin brand. Who calls a traditional brand Virgin? After all, it's an airline, it's a record store, it's a phone, and it's an entertainment company. If we are to believe the Virgin Web site, it's also a travel company, a healthcare company, and a financial service firm. It pretty much forces us to talk about it, just to begin to figure out what it is. What is it most often, day in and day out? It's in your face with audacious marketing tactics, an aggressive founder cum spokesperson, and branding by a seemingly whimsical, nearly free association sensibility, rather than by classic brand expansion strategies, namely, moving into logical bordering categories.

Virgin reportedly will enter an industry only if it believes it can challenge existing rules and give customers a better break, be more entertaining, and put a thumb in the eye of complacent competitor incumbents. One memorable ad for Virgin Air during the British Airways strike read, "British Airways Can't Get It Up."

The Virgin brand reminds me of a game of "What If," as in, "What if we did a series of creative brainstorms in a conference room and came up with all the things a brand could be—all id and no stern business superego to rein us in?" Interestingly, the businesses that Virgin has entered parallel many of General Electric's, which also seems to brand by free association. It's just that GE's offerings come to us minus the wit, minus the attitude, minus the edge, minus the devil-may-care disregard for convention, minus the willingness to be bold, brash, and brazen—and, therefore, minus the buzz.

A brand as staid and practical as IKEA can use the sizzle of smart-alecky advertising to provide some edge. In a British TV spot, a Swedish psychologist explained that the English are bad tempered because of English furniture, advising viewers to "Stop being so English." In another spot, a management consultant contemplates the enhanced furniture budget a corporation could earn by simply firing an additional office worker. In the United States in 1994, IKEA used what was believed to be the first gay couple in television advertising, shopping for home furnishings. It ran only once, creating a furor disproportionate to the advertising expense and creating millions of dollars of positive and negative word of mouth.

Some brands seek the high-voltage charge to power their marketing so eagerly that they change the rule book, courting controversy just to be the topic du jour of the chattering classes. These brands border into a world of brand gossip, the shivers of "Wait till you hear this" more usually used for rumor-mongering about people. Such chat may titillate some like the cover of a *US Weekly*, or Page Six of the *New York Post*, but it doesn't rise to the level of passion. Remember No Excuses Jeans? No? Well, that's exactly the point. This brand tied itself to tabloid newsflashes—Donna Rice? Paula Jones?—and started feeling as desperate as an aging starlet.

Sony Ericsson played a controversy card in 2002, right after 9-11, when it launched in the United States one of the first cell phones to take pictures. Reportedly, the company hired a group of Scandinavian people to pose as tourists, standing in front of major objects of interest around New York City, such as the Empire State Building and Radio City Music Hall. As people walked by, the "tourists" stopped them and asked them to take their picture, using their cell phone. Beyond the oohs and ahhs of the fascinated passersby, there was an undercurrent of anxiety, picked up by the media. Who were these people taking pictures of famous landmarks? What was their agenda? Negative publicity ensued, but Sony Ericsson didn't blink from the street corner strategy: they courted the controversy, as if to prove an old canard that any publicity is good publicity.

Red Bull also rode the wave of controversy, in its earliest days, when the word on the street was that its main ingredient was derived from bull testicles.[8] The brand never sought to correct the story, deciding instead to build on the legend of the product's secret ingredient, albeit fictitiously. The rumor helped in part at least to explain Red Bull's funky taste, as well as its boost to partiers' staying power in nightclubs and truckers' drive-through-the-night endurance. To confront the taste and conquer it became a rite of passage, a matador and bull (beverage) moment that, if not exactly worthy of Hemingway, certainly echoed him at the turn of the twenty-first century. A recent study of dangerous teen behavior cites preference for energy drinks as an early indicator of troubled times ahead.[9]

"Our driving idea was to use the oldest and best media in the world—word of mouth," says Norbert Kraihamer of Red Bull. "We were not about building mass distribution, but bases of consumers."[10] It used a disciplined microcell expansion strategy to limit availability with precision. Called "seed, weed, feed, and breed," the process calls for seeding a geography's bars with Red Bull, weeding out the locations that don't perform well for the brand, feeding the ones that do, and allowing the patrons of those bars to take the brand with them, breeding new congenial locations.

In the United States, Red Bull started in California: Santa Cruz and from there to San Francisco, then to Venice Beach,

Santa Monica, and Hollywood. "When one small cell became a success story, we moved onto the next cell. Of course, after three years, these cells [became] bigger and bigger. But initially it was towns or part of towns," says Kraihamer. Ultimately it expanded to the Rockies until the company established eight separate business units to manage the growth, which is beyond geographic and is becoming postdemographic.

Interestingly enough, another beverage phenomenon that started about the same time, Starbucks, used a comparable expansion strategy. In 1991 Starbucks entered Southern California, opening small kiosks in Hollywood, Beverly Hills, and West Los Angeles, followed by freestanding stores in Santa Monica, Brentwood, and Los Angeles. There was no location-specific advertising, but word of mouth worked to create lines outside the stores. David Lynch and Paula Abdul came. The *Los Angeles Times* dubbed Starbucks the best coffee in the country and, as Schultz described it, "Starbucks became chic."

"The kids that are eighteen or nineteen years old and drink Red Bull in a nightclub have years of use ahead of them," says Kraihamer. "These same people will use it in the future as a sporting drink, or for driving, or as a conference drink because business meetings are always tiring."

One of the keys, however, was guaranteeing that the shocking first taste of the product was well managed: sweet and carbonate, but also medicinal tasting, it's best ingested ice cold. Price was another element to signal its difference from Coke, Pepsi, and anything else that's out there: Red Bull seeks to sell for 10 percent more than the most expensive alternative. It is, after all, selling energy, or renewal, or reinvigoration, or another hour to a night; it is not selling refreshment.

"We have to make sure that people experience the product the right way at the right moment and in the right situation when they have met with particular fatigue or are in need of food," says Kraihamer. Presumably, at the right temperature, too. They used student teams, called Red Bull Student Managers, who went wherever consumers need the lift that a Red Bull provides: concerts, parties, festivals, sporting events, beach parties, highway rest areas, and campus libraries.

The brand also created new events to sponsor, like the Red Bull Soapbox Race and the Red Bull Flugtag (Flying Day), a funny event—even if you simply watch the highlights online—Snowthrill extreme skiing competitions and cliff diving world tour finals. It also worked with proven athletes, sponsoring them as individuals, making sure that they were authentic users of the product. The brand sought action sports: surfing, snowboarding, skydiving, skateboarding, rock climbing, and mountain biking.

Red Bull knew that limited distribution would generate bootlegging into new markets and hoarding in existing locales. The brand waited before moving on to ensure that consumers were creating a devoted following. Part of that devotion stemmed from the transgressive nature of the rumors about the brand. When Red Bull became associated with drug overdoses and deaths because of its clubber following, it never varied from its strategy of letting the consumers buzz about the brand (true or false, it was all buzz).

Arguably, a new study's findings, which suggest a correlation between the willingness to drink lots of Red Bull (and other energy beverages) and a predilection to exhibiting a "toxic jock" condition, a collection of risky and aggressive behaviors including unprotected sex, substance abuse, and violence may further heighten its appeal.[11]

There is reportedly a "Red Bull mystique." Kraihamer calls it the overmystification of Red Bull. Its development was spontaneous but not unpremeditated. The brand knew which markets it was going to launch in and prior to those launches, it would do what it calls "premarketing," including the sponsorship of events in countries where Red Bull was yet to become available. Local television programs covered the events and interviewed Red Bull endorsing athletes, but still there was nothing to buy just yet. As Kraihamer tells it, "We want to be recognized as the preeminent brand, even if we are not there."

The under-the-radar techniques went after cultural elites in shops, clubs, bars, and stores. Red Bull wanted to reach the people who reach people: athletes, celebrities, the hip, and the restless. But the Red Bull marketing edit is clear: "We do not market the product to the consumer, we let the consumer discover the product first and then the brand with all its image components," says Kraihamer.

That said, there was plenty that was buzzworthy about the brand's advertising. Imagine Dracula being told by his dentist that his teeth must be removed. Dracula bemoans his fate: "But without fresh blood my body will wither and my mind will fade." Oh, no, explains the dentist. "One revitalizing Red Bull and you'll be prince of the night again." The dentist then drinks it and tells Dracula, "You know, Red Bull gives you wings," then grows wings and soars off. Prince of the night. Again.

Here's another controversial approach to marketing refreshments: Mark DiMassimo and Eric Yaverbaum, head of Ericho Public Relations, longtime collaborators and friends, launched Tappening in 2007. Self-funded with a budget of less than two hundred thousand dollars, the brand was able to build buzz so quickly that by the end of the year, *Good Morning America* had named Tappening as one of the "Hot Products of 2008." What is the product? It's the idea (coupled with some well-designed water bottles) that tap water is a more ethical thirst quencher than branded bottled water.

DiMassimo and Yaverbaum consider Tappening to be a "movement" first and a brand and business second. They consider themselves to be "social entrepreneurs," or business-people with a motive to promote socially worthwhile values and behaviors through a profitable enterprise.

"A movement is the possession of its members," says DiMassimo. One of Tappening's great breakthroughs came when a few of the movement's activists sent the pair empty Dasani water bottles with pro–tap water messages enclosed. The two were inspired to launch a "Send a Message in a Bottle" campaign that generated hundreds of thousands of bottles delivered to incoming Coke CEO Muhtar Kent in July 2008. According to DiMassimo, once the bottles were sent to Kent and fifty other senior executives, "Coke wisely declined to comment."

Commerce takes a backseat to community, education, and activism on the Tappening.com Web site, according to DiMassimo. Yet, business is great, and the partners have been able to funnel a quarter of a million dollars of profits back into promoting tap water consumption through advertising, public relations, educational initiatives with schools, and support for the film *Garbage: The Revolution Begins at Home*, a new feature-length documentary by filmmaker Andrew Nisker.

When concerns arose over potential safety concerns related to BPA plastic bottles, Tappening communicated actively with members of the movement and quickly sourced non-BPA bottles and introduced stainless steel bottles as well.

A brand that discovered the painful dark side of the courting controversy theory is, of course, Camel. "When we launched Camel No. 9," Cressida Lozano explains, "the word of mouth far surpassed anything we'd ever seen. It just spoke to smokers in a loud way: fun, irreverent, confident. The black pack with the fuchsia Camel not only reinforced our fun, irreverent identity, but opened a door to competitive female adult smokers who until Camel No. 9 had not been able to find a Camel product that appealed to them. This bold new Camel got smokers talking, which was great.

"But several outspoken critics grabbed hold of it and accused us of targeting young girls, which of course we were not. The press had a field day."

While acknowledging that in some categories all news may well be good news, Mark Morrissey makes a terrific point: "For controversy to work as a marketing engine, it has to engender a spirited debate. We can't do that in this category any longer. The sides are too firmly entrenched. So we just stay away from it."

What Camel does instead to generate discussion is to consciously promote its "not-mainstream" status: Camel is simply not a mainstream choice. The decision to smoke in this epoch is a conscious one. The decision to smoke Camel is another conscious choice. So the brand nourishes its nonconformist roots. For example, in 2006 Camel commissioned artists to create new package art, "publishing" thirty-six different designs. Then it used white Camel packs in retail promotions, asking smokers to send in their own artwork, some of which were also published as Camel packages. These two promotions fit with the image of the brand as being the official cigarette of artists, poets, and musicians for generations.

The strictures under which tobacco brands operate make them a fascinating study in under-the-radar, grassroots tactics. Camel Bar Nights are a mainstay of clubs and bars in cities throughout the country, working both to give a friendly haven to smokers and to ensure that the brand's promotion targets only adults in age-restricted venues. Camel hires reps, or ambassadors, to serve as hosts in these settings. Smokers speak conspiratorially, even in whispers of Camel Bar Nights, as if giving out the address of a speakeasy during Prohibition.

At one point, Camel decided to create "invitation only"

events, welcoming all smokers, regardless of brand. "For smokers, it's just amazing at a time when they are often not welcomed," explains Cressida to me. "They say, 'Wow! Somebody's treating me special!' And for us, it's a time to talk one-on-one with smokers and tell them the story of our brand."

"What's important in this kind of grassroots dialogue," Morrissey adds, "is that you make it clear: I respect you; I respect the circumstances in which I meet you. I respect the fact that we're not just an advertising machine. We're people who share your enjoyment of tobacco."[12]

Buzz doesn't just have to be all attitude and controversy though: It can spread brand news like wildfire just because it ignites a powerful, underserved market. Think about how *High School Musical* surprised everyone, including Disney, with its tween appeal, spawning *High School Musical 2*, *High School Musical 1 and 2 on Ice*, and *HSM3* as a theatrical release. The idea at the beginning was just another made-for-Disney TV movie, but the preadolescent grapevine made it into a blockbuster franchise.

Another surprise for Disney was the street value of Hannah Montana concert tickets. Priced by the company to sell at around seventy-five dollars for the best seats on her fifty-city tour, they went for ten times that via resellers like Stub-Hub. Again, the pent-up demand for a talented fifteen-year-old with her own television series (and dual personality), cute boy opening act, sassy back-up singers, and charisma to spare generated the white heat of junior marketplace buzz and drove desperate parents to desperate measures. Yes, Mattie and I drove to Worcester, Massachusetts, from Manhattan to see Hannah Montana, who could not know she was the brokered alternative to a puppy for Mattie's eighth birthday.

Of course it's not just huge brands that benefit from buzz.

One example of this ethic at work is the recent phenomenon of *The Shack*, a book that began life as a story written by a father for his six children, using the shack as the metaphor "for the house you build out of your own pain."[13]

"He gave fifteen copies to his children and a few friends," according to an article in the *New York Times*. "When the friends wanted to send copies to other friends, [Paul] Young wondered if he might have something suited for a wider audience."[14] One year later, the manuscript has sold one million copies and is sold at WalMart and Costco, as well as Borders and Barnes & Noble. Reportedly, once someone buys it, they go back and get ten more for friends.

Amanresorts, that miraculous chain started in Thailand, is another brand that firmly admits to growth by buzz: According to Anthony Lark, one-time general manager of their flagship Amanpuri location, "Aman then was like the worst-kept secret. Adrian's friends told their friends and the word soon spread among a certain set who wanted privacy without pomp. Remember, this was at a time when the best these world travelers could find was a big, overly decorated suite in a hotel chain."[15]

This sense of a community that shares the same enjoyments and wants to talk about them was at the heart of the Crunch gym communication strategy, according to Mark DiMassimo. "Crunch competed in the entertainment category," he tells me. "It was a simple statement, but a huge advantage. So, if you went home to watch TV, we were there. If you went out to a nightclub, you'd likely find us on the bar napkins or in the restroom. Later, we branched out to places our target audience would most appreciate entertainment, which included airports and airplanes, too."[16]

A partnership with JetBlue Airlines, as an example, put punching bags in JFK International Airport with slogans such as "Middle Seat?" and "Missed Your Flight?" inviting passengers to work out their aggressions right there and then. In the seatbacks of all JetBlue flights were cards presenting "Airplane Yoga" and "Flying Pilates." The first of these was such a success that several arm rests were broken by overzealous passengers. A revision in the first reprinting saved the planes from further damage.

Thus, the creative measure for Crunch was "Is it entertaining? Is it buzzy? Is it no judgments? Is it Crunch?" The vision started with the entrepreneur behind it: "I'll only let you produce your best work, Mark," Doug Levine told DiMassimo. "Just make my drink spew out my nose." The work became so drink-out-the-nose audacious that Crunch posters and the gym itself were used in various television series to help telegraph character development. Meadow Soprano's Columbia University dorm room boasted a poster. *Will & Grace* built several episodes around a Crunch gym, and it was used in *Seinfeld*'s New York location, as well.

Crunch became famous for its huge events. Reality TV inspired one of the best: Rick Rockwell had been the prize on the first season of Fox's seminal *Who Wants to Marry a Millionaire?* The spectacle of a stage packed with women vying for his affection prompted one Crunch member to say, "Someone ought to kick that guy's ass." And off they went with a "Who Wants to Kick a Millionaire's Ass?" contest.

To promote Crunch's new and popular kickboxing aerobics classes, the contest became a three-ring circus of celebrity, media, and fisticuffs. The company asked gym members to nominate the "millionaire most deserving of an ass-kicking." Donald Trump and Bill Gates tied for first. This led to broad-ranging media speculation about who Crunch's millionaire would be. Rick Rockwell agreed to be the millionaire, in exchange for a twenty-five-thousand-dollar donation to his favorite charity and a five-minute extension to his fifteen minutes of fame. A twenty-two-year-old actress, Marni Rosenberg, won the right to kickbox the millionaire, replete with seemingly endless media coverage, including a prematch broadcast hosted by Howard Stern.

From a start-up idea, edgy with attitude, Crunch was sold fourteen years later to Bally's for $150 million: one more millionaire, but one fewer gym to kick his butt.

One of the tactics most typically used to connect with likeminded consumers is sponsorship—of races, rallies, concerts, street fairs. The people at the car manufacturer Scion explain their strategy: "We show up. That's it. We show up where our consumers are—because it's where we are, too. Sometimes it's our employees. Sometimes it's people we hire. But we don't sponsor anything that's out of line with our target."

To make the point, the brand has included a clause in its sponsorship contracts to ensure that if another sponsor signs on later and isn't edgy enough to be compatible, Scion can refuse to participate. They call this the "No Bayer Aspirin" cosponsorship rule. Similarly, on the brand's Web site, the focus is "discovered music," and once the group becomes popular, the brand moves on. The brand uses no mass media whatsoever. "We telegraph our content via our context," one Scion employee tells me, asking to be quoted anonymously and loathe to say more and ruin the magic.

Still, there's a serious marketing opportunity residing in the company's ability to connect in a symbiotic relationship with its devoted users. In a true passion brand culture, one with real passionistas engaged, we see what one writer terms the opportunity to provide subculture havens for its loyalists. The emphasis is not on simple sponsorships with banners and tents and pins and SWAG (the seemingly ubiquitous free stuff enshrined in goodie bags), but on becoming the consumer, as well as the marketer, blurring the line between maker and consumer and acknowledging a mutual, even tribal belonging. This step is easy enough to do for bikers, NASCAR, and fashion, perhaps. A bit harder if you're charged with marketing Bayer.

Red Bull sponsors hundreds of low-wattage events throughout the country, appealing to an eclectic celebration of weekend avocations from bikers to skateboarders to surfer dudes. The brand works hard not to look like big money: no publicity people, no signs, no sense of the scale and craft that goes into stage managing small but focused enthusiast gatherings in difficult to get to geographies every weekend of the year.

So brand marketing moves beyond the constraints of paid advertising, beyond television, radio, and print, and into reality: "Welcome to the brave new world of ConsumerSpace," writes Michael Solomon in *Conquering Consumerspace*. "Where reality is branded, where life and commerce are increasingly indistinguishable and where we are what we buy—literally."[17] Need further proof? Consider that advertising space on body parts has been sold on eBay. Or how about the British advertising agency that paid five people eight hundred dollars each to legally change their names for one year to Turok after the fictional comic book and video game hero?

WHAT WE TALK ABOUT WHEN WE TALK ABOUT BRANDS

Brand the Buzz

Verbatim Consumer Quotes

"My girlfriend told me about it. That's how I heard about it first. Then somebody at work started talking about it—pretty much as excited by *Sex in the City* as my girlfriend. I'd never really cared for shows about New York City. I mean it's not like that's my life, but I did start watching. And then I'd be talking about it too. Pretty soon, we started planning to meet at each other's house to watch together. We'd tell the husbands and the kids that this was our show and we'd kick them out of the family room. I learned how to make Cosmos. It became part of our lives. We didn't miss an episode—and sometimes we'd even get together for a rerun. We just missed them and each other. Towards the end, there were probably six or seven of us each week. It was so much fun. I mean it's pretty much like our mothers used to feel about soap operas, I guess. But they never had Cosmos with *As the World Turns*. At least I don't think they did!"

"There's this one kind of bean and it's only available for a short time, so when they get it in they call me and I go over. They put some aside for me. It's that kind of thing. The guy explained it to me, why it's so exclusive, so I told him I always want to get two or three pounds of it. I've told my friends, too, and now they love it. So he puts some aside for them, as well. It's cool to be on 'the list,' you know."

"I don't know how I first heard about, but I heard from someone, or I saw a picture of a Mini Cooper, and I just wanted one. It just looked so cool. So I went to the dealer and I got on the list and he gave me some material about it and I read up on it and started, I don't know, to kind of study it and the design philosophy and I talked to some people about it. I mean if I hadn't had to get on the waiting list, I probably wouldn't have spent so much time learning about it, but I did. I had the time and I was obsessed about it. My friends were kind of intrigued at first, but then they thought I'd gone off the deep end, you know. But then, when I got the car and I could explain everything about it to them, how the tail lights had evolved, who inspired the original design, all that kind of stuff, they were kind of impressed, I think. I mean I think they were. Maybe they were just humoring me—but they all noticed how heads turn when we drive around in it. I think a couple of my buddies are going to end up getting one. I do."

"It's how they make the dessert wines in Germany. I mean those are some really spectacular wines. So clear. A lot of people say, 'Oh, I don't like sweet wines,' but these aren't sweet wines. These are Trockenbeerenauslese for heaven's sake. But these are the very best dessert wines in the world. I think of a great dinner and then bringing out a well-chilled bottle and tiny glasses and just regaling my friends with the legend and lore of this wine. It just finishes off a great evening, everyone gets involved with the tasting and I explain where it's come from and how it's made and how I discovered it—or who turned me on to it—I don't want to sound so egotistical here, but it makes for a great end to the evening. With brandy or cognac, your head gets muddy, but with a crisp dessert wine, it's just a great finish."

Chapter 9
MY PRESCRIPTION FOR BUILDING BRAND PASSION

One of the things that became obvious to me on this passion brand odyssey was that while these seven accelerators each had powerful and persuasive real-market illustrations, there was no single brand that illustrated all of them. First I wondered, would this not be the ideal prescription for a postmodern brand? Then I thought, perhaps there's a good reason no single brand encompasses them all.

Finally I decided to give it a try and to make the attempt from two perspectives. How would the accelerators apply to a new brand, perhaps something imported or burrowed so deeply into a niche that we'd never heard of it? And how would these rules apply to an old-time brand that had been around forever? My hope is to help those of you reading this book and wondering how (and perhaps which) rules apply to your brand's circumstances.

I'm a big believer in models. They help explain relationships, timing, and sequence. So, let's return to the model I've used throughout this book.

PASSION BRANDING PROCESS

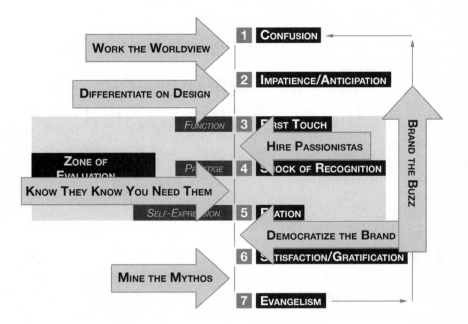

Once again, let me repeat my warning from the first chapter: the syntax I use here is a consumer experience syntax; it is not the way a company would actually develop a product, but rather how it should *reveal* it—unfurl it—over time to the consumer in order to engage his or her emotional commitment and ideally passion for it.

Let's imagine for the purposes of this chapter that you're importing a new skin care line from some exotic port of call, perhaps Thailand. This line is eco-friendly, made entirely from sustainable Thai ingredients; it's packaged in 100 percent recycled and recyclable paperboard; it has refillable containers. The formulations are based on the combination of the following: the product is based on the lay wisdom of the Thai people in its creation, indigenous plants and extracts that are used, and there is an affirmation of advanced skin care science available through the most sophisticated dermatological research. It's going to be priced comparably to specialty beauty products, such as those from Bath & Body Works or The Body Shop.

So far so good. As you walk through the various stores and aisles looking at the competition, you grasp the sense of confusion that must pervade the consumer experience. The same thing happens when you peruse fashion and beauty magazines or do Web searches. You're inundated by conflicting claims, solemn regimens, and beautiful packaging.

What to do? Determine first the *worldview of the consumer*. Could this be for both men and women? Could the environmental story appeal while the Thai ingredients and philosophy backstory provide a compelling reason for being? What sensory cues are necessary to ensure surprise and delight from the first usage, and ensure that you lock in the loyalty available through the refillable container tactic?

Perhaps we should start with small retail boutiques in Creative Class markets, such as New York, Los Angeles, and San Francisco, of course, but also Seattle, Austin, and Miami Beach, along with a savvy Web presence—one that will ultimately allow for consumer communities to emerge.

We work extremely close with the product design team in order to *differentiate on design*. Remember Steve Jobs's design discipline—make aggressively designed "I've just got to touch it" containers. We want nothing less than the Olivetti, iPod, or Michael Graves tea kettle of skin care products. They can look like nothing else out there, and yet they must look like they belong together.

Here's where consumer conversation is critically valuable: What are the unmet needs, the product disappointments in the current array of product packaging available at any price point? I use hypnosis to get at this, but I've also had success with consumer ideation sessions as well as Web-based conversations with communities of consumers who are passionate about this entire category. The idea of refillable containers is powerful, but there's a reason it hasn't been offered in this category before. It could be a nightmare from the consumer and store perspective, but is there a design solution to mitigate the hassle?

Now then, the help in the store. Who should be there? *Beauty passionistas*, of course. Who better to make the case intelligently, honestly, and, well, passionately? Should we use men and women? Why not? Do they wear some sort of uniform, perhaps something to connote the scientific credentials of the line, or perhaps something to suggest its origins? We need people who are beauty-regimen obsessed. How do we find them? We could recruit from the Fashion Institute of Technology and other respected beauty and cosmetics schools, perhaps from the armies of recent college graduates arriving every summer who want to break into retailing, fashion, and beauty; perhaps people with science or medical backgrounds; perhaps a combination. The guiding principle must be that they *want* to be doing this. They are excited to learn about the formulations; they are intrigued by the legend, lore, and science; they are proud of the earth-friendly elements to the story. They are going to be the equivalent of baristas, so we must ensure that there is a career path for them to pursue. This is not a way station en route to an acting job. This is what they'd be thinking about if they didn't work here.

Maybe we borrow from the hotel chains that offer every employee—*every* employee—a two-week vacation on any of their properties every year so they can experience the thrill of receiving the type of service they are expected to provide. Perhaps we'll send them for training to great spas or reward them after a year with a trip to the home office in Thailand.

No amount of service or packaging sizzle will allow us to sell a bad product twice. The product offerings here have to withstand the three-part rigor of the *zone of evaluation*: functional performance, prestige, and self-expression. We may be able to launch a line that covers one or two, but I'm convinced the only way to breed genuine passion is to hit all three.

The commitment of the passionistas can help educate consumers on how to evaluate the products, but it will be in the torture test of in-home usage that our fate is sealed. These three benefits need to be engineered into the line from the beginning. What are the functional performance benefits of each product, and how do we know we're getting them? Let's say that the lines all use folkloric ingredients fresh from the exotic terrain, augmented by scientific verification of their efficacy: legendary remedies and herbal treatments authenticated by people in white coats.

How can the consumer experience that? Sensory cues are the most significant. Smell, touch, and visual appeal: all take the reputed benefits and make them come alive. Beyond the design differentiation of the containers, how does the formulation of the product illustrate its story credibly? Is there the equivalent of wine labeling, perhaps, that tells the origin, vintage, and varietal? These formulations are made from organic ingredients; should we have the courage to admit that every crop of every plant matures differently every year?

Next, what prestige value does the brand embody? The eco-friendly elements of the brand are powerful support here. The brand is articulating a highly differentiated proposition when we compare it to all the overpackaged goods on the shelves today.

Next, what self-expression will the brand allow me? What am I saying with it—that I don't rely on the usual products, but have rather searched for nontraditional, unconventional sources of good skin care? I've discovered something fabulous and I want to tell you about it?

Once the consumer is moved to elation, how do we *acknowledge we know we need them*? One way surely is in interesting and folkloric events in the retail settings, after-hours events to which they can bring friends and try new products in a meditative and serene atmosphere. Certainly we can do this through the tone and voice of our marketing materials. These are thoughtful, even tranquility-inducing products developed for a conscious consumer by people who care deeply about people, the products, and the planet. In every name, package, benefit, sign, flier, e-mail, and interaction with retail staff, that welcoming yet intense worldview must come through: we can't do this alone.

That level of engagement must lead to the *brand's democratization*. One way is through consumer community–based activities on the Web. If Threadless can have people submitting T-shirt designs and voting on them, surely we can offer our consumers the opportunity to influence the fragrance, packaging, and brand-naming conventions for us. Container refill nights might be fun and focusing. Perhaps a gift registry? Perhaps not. Maybe customized packaging for homes, swag bags, and wedding party favors? Maybe not. What do they think?

The *mythic backstory* pretty much takes care of itself here. The challenge may be rendering it into sound bytes able to be heard, learned, and told. It's a big story. What part of it do we want to tell? What is our vocabulary? Is the eco-friendly aspect most important? The Thai authenticity? The raw beauty of the products? My vote would be to tell it all gracefully and let consumers decide how they want to talk about the products and then listen to that, digesting it and playing back the vocabulary they use to find and share the story.

The *buzz will be branded* by the total consumer experience the line provides at every step. How does the patron feel upon entering the shop, while in it, when touching the products, when talking about each one with staff, when carrying the bag out, when unpacking it at home and marveling again at its design, deciding to showcase it on the bathroom vanity rather than closeting it inside the cabinet, or when someone asks, "What are you wearing?" When she evaluates the regimen's performance on her sometimes oily, sometimes dry skin, when she is invited back to the store for an event, when the staff person is still there three years later and remembers her, when she reads about their product line in *Allure*, and yes, when she recommends it passionately to friends.

The genuine passion brand reveals itself at every step along this path. That's why it's worth talking about.

The torture test of passion branding may well be the low-involvement world of the grocery store, working with packaged goods products. I remember when Nabisco owned Fleischmann's margarine and one of the executives told me that the average consumer decision time for margarine was two seconds: One second to reach into the case; one second to pull the product out. No time devoted for contemplating a new brand choice.

Now, of course, the category had done this to itself. The reason we don't stutter when we look in the margarine section is that there is no product news there. Off and on there is product-related news, as in margarine is good for us, or margarine is bad for us, and then margarine is good for us again. It seesaws back and forth but not because of anything the manufacturers do, just because dietary science is both messy and newsworthy. One day's health scare is tomorrow's boon.

As part of our work on the brand, we did a series of expert panels involving all sorts of professionals from many realms: science and medicine, packaging, marketing, manufacturing, distribution, news media, and even parenting. Essentially we were casting a wide net to try to figure out how to slow that buying process down, to make it into a decision process again rather than simple rote behavior. What would it take?

The answers we came up with were never able to be tried in the market because Nabisco sold the Fleischmann's brand before we had the chance to implement any new marketing approach. But it's always stuck with me as a great example of what could have been developed for this famous mark.

During one of the expert groups, we invited some people from Nabisco's research and development division. One was an extremely bright and earnest young fellow who volunteered at one point something he probably thought everybody knew, but we surely didn't. "You know there are such things as fat-soluble vitamins," he said, almost in passing.

The idea captured the imagination of everyone in the room, and we began to build on the concept. What if Fleischmann's became the preferred carrier of all those vitamins we think we're getting in pills, but which all the dietitians and nutritionists kept telling us simply made for "really expensive urine," since our bodies didn't metabolize them. The product concept just kept getting larger and larger: ages and stages would need different levels of these fat-soluble vitamins. Suddenly, the vision of shelf-sets emerged, laid out as logically and beautifully as L'Eggs pantyhose dispensers or Granimals in their heydays.

Since I didn't get to work on this in real life, imagine with me how dusty old Fleischmann's might have emerged a passion brand.

Worldview: Health-involved adults, their children, and their parents. (This group would almost be as large a target audience as that envisioned for Red Bull.)

Differentiation on Design: It would have been so much fun to have worked with world-class designers to develop the whole look, cueing consumers immediately to just the right product for each member of the family. The one for the elderly might have had easy-open, easy-pour spouts. Pregnant women? Puberty stricken teens? No problem.

Hire Passionistas: This would be pretty difficult, really. The Nabisco sales guys might have been excited, but how would we get the check-out clerks engaged? The best way around this one might have been to hire and train local experts to conduct miniseminars in the aisle at key times of the day, educating consumers about the new product's benefits as well as conducting tastings and sampling recipes using the product. The key thing about food is that no matter what else it is claimed to do, it has to taste good. So we'd have taste reassurance right at the point of purchase.

Acknowledge They Know We Need Them: The tone of voice would have to be crucial. Vitamins, even well-metabolized ones, aren't the holy grail of lifelong health. But among key audiences we would have worked to engage them with stories of the small triumphs the brand now enabled. We're not providing a silver bullet in the form of margarine fortified with fat-soluble vitamins, but we are looking for ways consumers have embraced a total healthy life, of which we're a part.

Brand Democratization: What else would customers like in the margarine category? Once we've opened up the shelf to actual shopping—actually making a choice between margarines—are there other forms and perhaps flavors, maybe some with other health-related benefits, that would continue to surprise and delight? Could antioxidants be a part of our story? Are there events we could also attend? Could there be some limited-edition flavors, based on harvested ingredients that are available for short seasons? For small batches without great mass appeal, should we offer to direct-mail quantities to the devoted?

Mythic Backstory: The anecdotal joy of the young

researcher's excited sharing of fat-soluble vitamins seemed to be the type of story we all love. I would have started with that, ensuring that the young fellow stayed involved every step of the way, perhaps even suggesting him as product spokesperson. Who better to articulate the eureka moment? Supporting him with groups of experts to ensure legitimacy of the nutritional and dietary credentials to deliver a sustaining level of new advances would have made this a powerful passion brand.

Branding the Buzz: Plenty to talk about here, from nutritional realities to customizing classic recipes. There would be no shortage of things to say about Fleischmann's and why we buy it, serve it, and evangelize about it.

But, alas! That didn't happen.

Still, I encourage you to follow these steps to what could happen, for you, your fledging idea, the avocation you'd like to make a vocation, your hopes for the businesses you're working in today. My wish for you? Work with passion. Indeed, become a passionista, wherever you find yourself right now.

Part Two

WHY NOW?

Chapter 10
THE AGING OF US

There seem to be two driving cultural forces at play in our world today that make this crucible of passion brand alchemy possible, as mere things begin to have powerful personal relationships with us. First, there are crucial, immutable, demographic trends that send us toward the safe harbor of powerful brands, the key one being aging.

Well, yes, we are getting older.

It might be better just to skip this chapter, particularly if you're a boomer or younger. We like to belittle the advent of Botox, wrinkle-reducing serums, and endless fitness regimens as proof that this country is in denial about aging, that we treat it as a predicament in need of a cure.

Right now in the United States there are roughly sixty million people older than fifty-five, and the nation's median age is forty-three. In other words, half the population is younger than forty-three and half are older. This large baby boomer group is, indeed, the elephant in the python. But it's the boomers' parents, the eighty-five-plus age group, that is the fastest-growing segment of the population. Scores of books, articles, and presentations laud the spending power of these mature folks. The current senior population possesses more than $900 billion in spending money, according to one assessment. They spend an estimated $30 billion on travel each year. That kind of thing gets bandied about.

That's not what I'm talking about here. Not the strength of their portfolios, but the strength of their worldview, their experience, their wisdom.

Betty Friedan's *The Fountain of Age* puts forth her "cure," based on a realization made as she researched the book: "I began to recognize some new dimension of personhood, some strength or quality of being in people who had crossed the chasm of age and kept on going and growing."[1]

Psychologically, sexually, and financially the "keep on going and growing" may well be, but physically, well, we're on a slippery slope. Age does present a series of sensory diminutions. Our senses are the way we get information about the world and once we pass forty, those senses become less and less acute. My theory here is that passion brands give us ways to renew our sense of our own currency at a time when wee bits of us are shutting down.

Basically, there's a threshold that a phenomenon is required to reach before we notice it. As we get older, the threshold increases. It takes more input before we become conscious of stimulation. That deterioration is sometimes accompanied by a sense of isolation, which from a passion brand perspective provides the opportunity to connect emotionally with *a thing*, particularly a favored thing, and more precisely a celebrated, adored, and relied-on thing.[2]

Let's go through the list of aging events. Hearing loss, vision, taste, smell, then touch seems to be the order of erosion; all exacerbated by lifestyle choices, such as choice of music, smoking, recreational drug use, binge drinking, and other high-risk behaviors.

Hearing loss starts about age fifty, particularly for people who attended lots of high-decibel rock concerts in their youth, or perhaps they still like to witness the occasional Rolling Stones reunion, Grateful Dead raucous caucus, or Madonna's latest incarnation. It seems the auditory nerve starts to go, making it difficult to take sound and turn it into evocative information.

Nearly everyone older than fifty-five needs some kind of assistance seeing clearly for some part of the time, particularly, it seems to me, in romantically lit restaurants when perusing the menu. There's this flash of glasses coming out of purses and suit jacket pockets that is a silent but nearly universal testimony. We begin to lose our peripheral and night vision, too.

The senses of taste and smell are the inextricably entwined ones that tell us about our food choices. For women from age forty to fifty and for men age fifty to sixty, the nine thousand taste buds they've relied upon begin to decrease and the remaining ones start to lose their sensitivity and acuteness. We'll lose salt and sweet tastes first; bitter and sour tastes remain longer. The loss of nerve endings in the nose makes smell a sense that erodes in our eighties. In addition, our mouths make less saliva, which makes swallowing tricky, digestion less efficient, and dental problems more frequent.

Then, of course, there's touch and physical sensation. As we age, there's decreased blood flow to various places in the body that process these feelings: touch receptors, brain, and spinal cord. There's also a reduced ability to feel pain, which is problematic. As is our compromised ability to recognize the difference between hot and cold, which can result in frostbite, hypothermia, and burns.

Add to this litany a variety of prescription drug interactions that can further compromise our senses' ability to give us information, and it begins to start feeling like sixty isn't "the new forty" after all. (I did warn you about this chapter.)

And yes, there is the fact that as we age our brain chemistry starts to shift a bit. We're not making as much serotonin, a compound in our blood that acts on the brain to promote feelings of personal security, relaxation, and confidence. The scientific community is just getting a handle on the biochemical reasons why certain disorders escalate with age: depression, anxiety, insomnia, and an urge to overeat are but the most frequent tribulations associated with serotonin deficiency.

There's a sad gravitational momentum as we age. It's a movement toward isolation, with impaired communication and sensory skills exacerbating the process. Thus, the antigravitational tug of passion brands becomes more pronounced in our age. We're getting older; our senses are *not* getting better. Okay. We get it. So what do we do? We seek the adventure of new experiences that must inevitably escalate if they are to have the desired impact. We look for shocking moments to interrupt the day-to-dayness we fear our lives have settled into.

Just witness the rise in "fiery condiments," which has grown into a business worth more than $3.5 billion in just the past ten years. That's a lot of sweet onion mustards, chipotle chili mayonnaises, zesty garlic ketchups, plus grilling sauces, marinades, dips, salsas—and even a concoction called Original Pit Bull Hot Sauce, the sweet sauce that BITES YOU BACK. Add to this the $500 billion market for ethnic foods, at home, in restaurants, and on-the-go. Our taste buds need excitement!

Safe shocks that disrupt without truly disturbing come from passion brands that provide harmlessly transgressive tropes to help separate us from our worst fears of humdrum existence. They help us declare that we're involved in making interesting choices.

Even the youngsters among us are aging, albeit a bit belligerently. They bring Red Bull to the conference room. They're loathe to give up their MacWorld habits when they enter heretofore Windows-centric corporate America, thereby bringing the cool factor they've grown up with along for the ride.

We recalibrate, process new information, and move toward exciting experiential products for which we don't have to struggle in front of people to read the small type in the instruction manuals. Passion brands give us something to converse about with self-assurance because they are so practical yet original. We talk about them as personal anecdotes—movies, grocery delivery services, dining experiences, airlines, vodka— without having to demonstrate immediate mastery of them. Yes, we can share stories of how difficult the plasma screen TV was to install, but we're highlighting the bliss of the resulting home theater.

Chapter 11
THE NEW ISOLATIONISM

We may be wired, but we are also untethered. We are becoming increasingly disengaged from the real-time world around us. We multitask in every phase of our lives—walking down the street, listening to our own music, breaking out of this cocoon only to talk on the cell phone, systematically ignoring check-out people, passersby, and the reality that everyone isn't equally interested in the details of our job, love life, or mother-in-law's behavior.

There's a fair amount of academic literature suggesting strongly that we are literally rewiring ourselves, our brains, to be able simultaneously to stay connected and keep people at bay, the twin facets of modern communications technology.

If we take a quick look at communications history, we'll see that we've always done it. That is, we've found ways to communicate for three distinct benefits: connection, avoidance, and corruption. When speech was our only means of communicating, we were limited by the strength of our voice. We could connect only with those within our range. We found ways to avoid face-to-face conversations by crossing the street, becoming obviously involved in some other task, like window shopping or fabricating an appointment that called us away from an extended conversation. If we wanted to, we could corrupt other people's communication via eavesdropping, gaining gossip for its self-aggrandizing or social power advantage.

When writing was added to the messaging mix, new limits were established. The sound barrier was crossed, although mail ships could sink, the Pony Express could be robbed, and in any event the financial cost to send things to others was high. Recipients could delay in opening, delay in responding, or they could ignore the letter altogether. But written communication offered a way to avoid giving bad news in person; whether to terminate a romance or a job, it served as a social screen. And it allowed for the creation of a new (if not exactly true) sender persona and the possibility that the recipient could share it with people for whom it was never intended.

The advent of information and communication technologies simply exacerbated this law of connection, avoidance, and corruption (CAC). We moved first to telephones, and with the introduction of voice-mail came a variety of ways to control connection. Call waiting enabled us to "stand by" in order to gain the object of our attention's attention, sooner rather than later. Equally, such technology provided the means of avoidance. Voice-mail means we can leave messages. Automated answering systems and their associated phone trees, with one extension after another, mean we have no prayer of speaking to anyone ever within most corporations. Caller ID technology allows us to avoid or even block unwanted callers endlessly. With the growing use of speakerphones, no caller can ever really know how many people may be listening in.

When e-mail arrived, CAC only escalated. We respond when we want to, with as much or little detail as we like. We can broadcast the message to as many people as we want. We can in many cases be whomever we want to be, as anyone who's actually met someone they've chatted with on an online dating site will certainly attest.

Then there's instant messaging (IM) with its buddy lists ("away even when we're not" messages) and endless ability via allowing calls to go direct to voice-mail and ignoring e-mails until we're ready (or can credibly deny receipt, if it comes to that)—all tactics to avoid in-person communication on any serious topic.

Let's not forget the cell phone, with its ring tones, text messaging, and camouflage services that make it plausible to say, "Sorry, there's so much traffic, I'm going to be late" while you're still at home in your pjs or pretending to be fielding a really important call that's interrupting this one.

When we cobble all this together, we get the modern-day multitasking platform, from which it's extremely difficult for anyone to know that you're doing something else while you're allegedly paying attention to them. Multitasking isn't new either, of course. We've done it forever. We're aware of the demands of driving a car: steering, watching in front of us, checking the rearview mirror, checking the periphery. All of these are cognitive tasks that we must manage simultaneously, perhaps with the added kicker of talking on the phone, listening to music, or paying attention to our child's story from the playground. Most studies insist that multitasking degrades the specific performance of any single task, whether it's specifically cognitive or social. Thus, we may be better off when we're not overloading ourselves with multiple activities.

That may be all well and good, but the fact is we are all multitasking all the time, with the trade-offs becoming factored in as part of our personal calculus. If we do it well, we can add another seven hours to our day, according to one British study.

If we do it poorly, well, we're in a car accident or we find our-selves having irretrievably sent a nasty comment in an e-mail to someone on the "CC" list who really, really, really shouldn't have gotten it. Or even worse, we utter a distracted "uh huh" when a close friend tells us her marriage is over. We're juggling and every once in a while, a ball gets dropped.

It's the social aspect of multitasking—beyond the cognitive performance issues it raises—that intrigues as it relates to the potential implications for brands, particularly the rise of passion brands. Stephen Brown hypothesizes right along with me: "Per-haps brands are providing the friendship, the social linkage that's becoming increasingly rare in our atomized society. I'm thinking of that book *Bowling Alone*," he writes to me.

The book he refers to is Robert Putnam's treatise on how we've become more and more severed from family, friends, and neighbors as well as the body politic. His evidence? Nearly half a million interviews over the last twenty-five years show that we sign fewer petitions, belong to fewer organizations that actually have meetings, get together with friends less often, and socialize with family sporadically. We are, in his term, bowling alone. The reasons: suburban life, television, computers, as well as the aging of the population and changes in family structure and women's roles.[1]

Researcher Naomi S. Baron, author of *Always On*, looks to the Amish for an alternative to the "always on, always con-nected" lifestyle promised by Blackberry advertising. We may imagine the Amish approach to modern products as parallel to the anti-industrial, Luddite movement of the British textile union artisans in the early nineteenth century, whose dissent was often punctuated by the destruction of mechanized looms. The modern Amish, she writes, use disposable diapers, gas barbecue grills, and even some diesel-powered machinery. The key to adoption? "Each new contrivance must be evaluated by the Amish bishops, with one fundamental query in mind: 'Does it bring us together, or draw us apart?'"

Their view of a forbidden home telephone: "What would that lead to? We don't want to be the kind of people who will interrupt a conversation at home to answer a telephone. It's not just how you use the technology that concerns us. We're also concerned about what kind of person you become when you use it."[2]

Baron uncovers a telling anecdote about what kind of a people we have become when she highlights an article in the *New York Times* written by David Carr about his new video iPod. "Last Tuesday night, I took my place in the bus queue for the commute home. Further up the line, I saw a neighbor— a smart, funny woman I would normally love to share the dismal ride with. I ducked instead, racing to the back of the bus because season one of the ABC mystery-adventure *Lost* was waiting on my iPod."[3] That's who we run the risk of becoming, a solitary bowler.

Kevin Kelly, former executive editor of *Wired* magazine, points us in a more optimistic direction when he says that some of the technorati are beginning to create rules of the road to reduce the wear and tear on our social fabric caused by information and communication technology. Not doing personal e-mailing from work is one, augmented by the other side of the coin, turning off the Blackberry once you cross the threshold at home.

Clearly, netiquette and etiquette must merge. A 2006 ABC study of rudeness in America ranks people talking loudly on cell phones in public places as the number one most frequent complaint.[4] Another study says that multitasking is rude on its face when it involves talking to someone on the phone while doing something else like e-mail or texting, because the other person can feel left out, unattended, or simply "dissed." A

Sprint study reported that 50 percent of people have a sense of "personal abandonment" when a friend or colleague paused in a face-to-face conversation to answer a cell phone.[5] A Hewlett-Packard study said that 89 percent of office workers were irritated by the behavior of colleagues who sent e-mails or text messages during meetings.

In a blog on geek etiquette, one writer reported on multi-tasking manners: "I mentioned the fact that geeks at conferences all sit using their laptops right through the presentations. 'I hate that,' opined one of my lunch companions. 'It's so rude. If they're not paying attention at all, what are they doing there?' I did a double take and then explained carefully. Geeks multitask. Not only do we multitask . . . what many of us are doing while we're staring at our laptop screens is sitting on IRC [Instant Relay Chat] on a channel dedicated to the conference and talking about the presentation in progress."

Imagine giving a presentation to a room filled with people checking their laptops, Blackberries, and cell phones for incoming messages, Googling for more information on the topic you're discussing; keeping up with office work and gossip; and critiquing in live chat rooms about your style, facts, interpretation, and delivery. What a turnoff for the speaker and for those in the audience trying to listen.

Beyond the lack of eye contact and concentration from the audience for a presenter, netiquette—or lack thereof—poses problems for corporations and individuals in scores of situations. There are some common standards that have evolved, such as, don't use ALL CAPS in e-mails, because it reads like shouting. E-mail, IMing, and to a lesser extent, chat room postings, may seem to be relatively private, but examples of notorious violations abound. Remember when Paris Hilton's Sidekick PDA was hacked, resulting in personal photos and address book entries being published on the Web?

Another example comes from the CEO of Cerner, Neil Patterson.[6] Regarding Cerner, a healthcare information technology company, and its work ethic, Patterson wrote to staff, in part, "The parking lot is sparsely used at 8 A.M.; likewise at 5 P.M. As managers—you either do not know what your EMPLOYEES are doing; or YOU do not CARE . . . in either case, you have a problem and you will fix it or I will replace you!"

According to a Wikipedia entry, "After the e-mail was forwarded to hundreds of other employees, it quickly leaked to the public. On the day the e-mail was posted to Yahoo!, Cerner's stock price fell by over 22 percent from a high of $1.5 billion."

Even something as old-school as CC/BCC e-mail functions can lead to horrible consequences, as when the Department of Homeland Security used a CC list in place of a mailing list to send messages to hundreds of recipients. Those people then misused the "reply to all" response to expand the e-mail to 2 million messages, which brought down the mail server.

So, we have the erosion of personal relationships that multitasking causes. One more example, this time from the Sunday edition of the *New York Times*, in the Modern Love column: "I was no stranger to Andy's all-consuming jobs, but now his work had begun to consume our family. He would routinely enter the house at night with a finger to his lips so no one would greet him while he finished a work call. . . . I became the quintessential insulting spouse, maligning him in advance of an anticipated slight."[7]

We have the erosion of our social interaction with colleagues and even strangers who don't want to overhear the details of our lives. There's the erosion of privacy of our correspondence, which can be published into the blogsphere in a nanosecond. We even call ourselves "addicted" to our "Crackberries" in an effort to acknowledge the obvious, as well as to distance ourselves from the problem via humor.

But what kind of people are we becoming as we use these devices? They are not going to go away. But we need to concede the subtle and not-so-subtle impact of these devices on us—and the implications for the marketplace.

Impact: We're losing valuable social skills and becoming a narcissistic, mechanized "segment of me." Therefore, we crave connection; we need help with social engagement; and we yearn for something interesting to talk about. Voilà, the GEICO gecko.

Chapter 12
THE AUTOMATON-IZATION OF REALITY

In the service of efficiency and productivity, we rely on software programs instead of people to do routine tasks, and we quite prefer the programs. From receptionists to bank tellers to sales clerks, the messy everyday dealing with inefficient strangers diminishes daily as we seek the safely robotic. Who would not rather plot an address in Mapquest than stop at a gas station to ask directions? Better yet, better to just have an "our lady of the dashboard" navigation system, as we call her, tell us how to get where we're going.

There's a thrill involved in automation of tasks formerly known as human, as when a friend takes you to a Wawa store for the first time in Philadelphia and shows you how to use their "built-to-order" hoagy and sandwich touch screen–ordering process. My sources tell me that kids drive forty-five minutes out of their way to find a Wawa just to avoid the hassle of a personal interaction with counter help at other convenience stores and quick-serve restaurants, which kind of redefines our understanding of the term "convenience" when you stop to think about it.

We've become intolerant of humanity's inefficiencies, demanding "right the first time" perfection, even at the cost of listening to Muzak and "your call is important to us" chants. What better to have for a friend than a brand, which in the best of cases has a distinct, entertaining, and status-conferring personality, and can be depended upon to "be there for me when I need it"? This descriptive phrase is the one consumers invariably use when they speak about "my favorite brand," whether it be Camel, Dove Chocolates, Sam Adams Beer and Ale, Starbucks, or Calgon.

There are social factors that push us toward an evolving sense of a personal, private community that uses brands as the "dog whistle" to signal membership. Historian Daniel Boorstin says that in the modern era of high mobility, people look beyond the neighborhood to form bonds based on consumption preferences. These *consumption communities*, as he termed them, are made "of people with a feeling of shared well-being, shared risks, common interests, and common concerns. These came from consuming the same kinds of objects: from those willing to 'Walk A Mile For A Camel,' those who wanted 'The Skin You Love to Touch' or who put faith in General Motors. The advertisers of nationally branded products constantly told their constituents that by buying their products they could join a select group, and millions of Americans were eager to join."[1]

While we're no longer in that era of mass indoctrination by brands, the psychological sense of community—unconnected by geography or time constraints—is a powerful force in the consumer economy we inhabit.

Convinced that all products are pretty much "okay, available, and cheap," we seek to be entertained by our brands, identified with our brands, connected through our brands. We crave fun, wit, and a shared sensibility with brands, through which we triangulate via brand telepathy to connect with other like-minded consumers. Thus, an iPodNation emerges.

The iPod, its advertising, and its image become the message we want to convey about ourselves. While the technology may have been groundbreaking initially, it's the image that commands we buy it and not some other MP3 version of it. "What does the use of this product say about me (the consumer)?" becomes the marketer's question to answer. It becomes about symbolic meaning once functional competence is a given.

Then there is the element of the marketplace in which we acquire the goods. Entering the Apple Store in New York City is akin to an excellent museum experience. There's the architecture, the well-lit display of products, the way the consumers seemed to have dressed for the part of Apple shopping—and of course the hush that descends over the entire enterprise. Perhaps not quite the Temple of Dendur but a worshipful experience, nonetheless. We're paying homage as well as buying.

This is where the hyperreality of the postmodern marketplace takes on its greatest import: hyperreality is well illustrated by the Second Life discussion in chapter 6. It's the concept that some things—like Disney's Magic Kingdom, Niketown, or the Apple Store—are more real than reality. Sometimes the distinctions between the real and hyperreal can become fuzzy. Stephen Brown, as usual, puts it well: "In certain respects, indeed, hyperreality is superior to everyday reality, since the negative side of authentic consumption's experiences (such as antitourist terrorism in Egypt, muggings in New York, or dysentery in Delhi) magically disappears when such destinations are re-created in Las Vegas or Walt Disney World. Ironically, however, the alleged superiority of the fake is often based on an unwarranted stereotype of the real, and the reality of the fake—standing in line in Tokyo Disneyland, for example—may be much worse than anything the average visitor would actually experience in Egypt, New York, or Delhi."[2]

We no longer simply consume a product; we consume its symbolic meaning. Insofar as we adopt the image that the product allows us to convey to our uses, we become its marketers. Of course, we assume the product works in a functional way; what we crave now is the aesthetic innovation and the self-definition that it brings. Technology serves to enable us to create images to tell our own story.

At its worst, we cast ourselves as bit players in a series of fictional narratives told by marketers: thin, fit people who enjoy an active lifestyle eat at McDonald's with their extraordinarily happy families. At its best, we take elements from the market and craft a unique, personal experience from them. We become a "protagonist in the customization of our world," according to one writer. It's my unique playlist, but I'm a member of the iPod tribe.

Thus, the consumer seeks to toggle between two poles and uses passion brands as the conduit: self versus community and images provided by the marketer versus images (experiences) constructed by the consumer. Marketers who "get it" are able to facilitate the movement of a product into a subculture community: skins, earbuds, and sound docks all amplify the signal of community membership.

Bernard Cova uses the Harley Owners Group (HOG) as an example, in an article in *Business Horizons*.

> Harley-Davidson marketers have maintained just such a relationship with HOG and diverse subgroups—or tribes of Harley-Davidson devotees. By understanding the process of self-transformation individuals undergo within the HOG subculture of consumption, these marketers can take an active role in socializing new members and cultivating the

commitment of current ones. Harley-Davidson marketing cultivates consumer commitment by providing a full range of clothing, accessories, and services that function as involvement-enhancing side bets and exit barriers.[3]

This new arrangement requires us to be not mere targets but rather producers of valuable experiences. Brand participation becomes the goal, transcending the mere purchase of a product. Taken to its logical conclusion, when we seek to understand the consumer, we do not just focus on assessing "need state fulfillment" but rather the consumer goal of experience creation.

Such brands simply vault over ironic narcissism to create a bond with us that is personal, permanent, and pervasive. It is so potent it inures the brands against price pressures, delivering both the demonstrable rational advantages and the unfathomable psychic benefits that mandate a committed relationship between brand and buyer, a relationship in which to a surprising degree both sides benefit.

"The fragmentation of society, made possible and fostered by the developments of industry and commerce, is among the most visible consequences of this postmodern individualism," Bernard Cova writes. "Products and services have progressively freed people from all alienating tasks left behind by tradition, even shopping itself. From one's own home, and without the necessity of a physical social interaction, one can obtain almost anything one desires. All the technology offered thus increases one's isolation while permitting one to be in virtual touch with the whole world. . . . The process of narcissism, induced by the development and widespread use of computers in all aspects of human existence, characterizes postmodern daily life."[4]

Emerging as an antidote to all this is the "Burning Man Project," the annual experience held in the Black Rock Desert near Reno, Nevada. Started in 1986 by Larry Harvey and a couple hundred others, it has become a themed event attracting twenty-five thousand or more each Labor Day weekend. The community that has sprung up around this seven-day adventure embraces an ethic of individuality, creativity, artistic expression, and irreverence—and yet the Burning Man Project has become just another brand, with strong cultural meaning, has it not? Ticket sales, posters, blogs, and a Web site all act together as a gravitational pull toward commerce that seems inexorable at this point.

Cova believes that the seeds of a "de-differentiation"—a coming together—have been sown in postmodern marketing. We do not, to use his term, "crown" the victory of the individual. Rather our epoch heralds a "desperate search for a social link." The word the majority of us have heard most often is brand "tribe" or "cult" to signal the return of such an old-world construct as community. And these communities, liberated via the Internet from the need for physical or time proximity, emerge and disperse since they are held together through emotion, lifestyles, moral beliefs, and consumption preferences.

These groups come together, creating their own symbols and rituals—think of groups of skinheads, Harry Potter aficionados, dancers, gamers, geeks, and the like—but we all belong to several different tribes at one time and many different tribes throughout a lifetime. This begins to erode our traditional view of social classes and configuration, as we take our place as a leader in one group and a neophyte in another.

Chapter 13

THE "OTHER PEOPLE WHO BOUGHT THIS BOOK ALSO LIKED . . ." IDENTITY

I mentioned that there is a "dog whistle" element to branding. By this I meant the notion that we send each other messages through our choice of brands. Our brand choices can be said in many ways to trump class and station, and in some ways to reinvigorate them as meaningful constructs.

The way they trump class and station: "What's great about this country is that America started the tradition where the richest consumers buy essentially the same things as the poorest," wrote Andy Warhol. "You can be watching TV and see Coca Cola, and you know that the President drinks Coca Cola, Liz Taylor drinks Coca Cola, and just think, you can drink Coca Cola, too. A coke is a coke and no amount of money can get you a better coke than the one the bum on the corner is drinking. All the cokes are the same and all the cokes are good. Liz Taylor knows it, the President knows it, the bum knows it, and you know it."

How do brands reinvigorate class and stature? Signature bags from Prada, Louis Vuitton, and Hermes suggest the process, as do their replica knock-offs. Or Rolex, Breitling, and Cartier watches, and their rip-off imitations do likewise. Watches are not just watches, and everyone knows it, even the bum on the corner who's trying to sell you a five-dollar imitation of one.

AMAZON.COM'S
RECOMMENDATION ALGORITHM APPLIED TO LIFE EVENTS.

BY MARIBETH MOONEY

Customers who had just broken up with their boyfriends
also had this happen:

A discovery of newfound freedom

An appreciation for having loved and lost

An intense desire for ice cream, vodka, and revenge

A charge of stalking and a subsequent warrant for their arrest

---

So we signal ourselves in these ways. We find it tremendously reassuring when Amazon suggests other books or DVDs we might like. If my favorite analyst, Dr. Richard Zimmer, is correct that Freud believed all we are really after at our root is "significance," then this Amazon computer assist—"People who liked this book also liked . . ."—is hardwired to please us. Both the significance of my purchase and the associated joy of being with like-minded others are compelling. The other consumers are like us. Thus, our opinions matter. Someone—albeit an algorithm—has bothered to notice.

The "Amazon.com recommends" feature is the one we're all most familiar with, I suspect. But Chemistry.com, Match.com, Netflix, and a wide variety of other dating and shopping sites have each pioneered their own algorithms to help us buy more things faster and (one hopes) better, helping us "be us," or at least find others like us. Why do we want to find others like us? Why wouldn't we want to see ourselves as unequally perceptive in seeing the value of a product, indeed that we're way ahead of the crowd, who will follow and appreciate our savvy, shepherded along by the algorithm?

Beyond the Amazon homepage recommendations area, the site analyzes our shopping cart, once we've starting shopping, to offer up the equivalent of the old-fashioned "impulse buy, getting us to consider something more in a flash." The Amazon algorithm is what is called an item-to-item collaborative filtering mechanism; it scales to take in huge amounts of data and suggests recommendations in nanoseconds.

The trick is that it's looking not at customer behavior but at item-to-item comparisons. It looks at the types of items usually purchased together and then seeks to make recommendations from those categories. Incredibly, it gets smarter as we shop, making virtually instantaneous modifications as we add each new thing to our cart.

Chapter 14
THE UBIQUITOUS MARKETING GENE

There is a certain redundancy in the fundamental message of this chapter and the viewpoint expressed in chapter 5, "Know They Know You Need Them." Nonetheless, I close with it here because it's such an important element of both the reason why passion brands have become so rooted in our culture and how they operate. The ubiquity of the marketing gene is both cause and cure.

YouTube.com, with its "Broadcast Yourself" tagline, is undoubtedly one of the best examples of what it means that we're incredibly marketing aware and indeed becoming marketers of self, sense, and sensibility. The technical term for this category is user generated content (UGC) and there can be no doubt it's remodeling the world of information and entertainment.

New viewer patterns have emerged and with them new forms of social engagement as well as new business models. Prior to this UGC insurgency, this type of content came from broadcasters and producers. It must be seen as the modern-day equivalent of the revolution wrought by the printing press. The only apparent limitation at the moment is one of time, in deference to bandwidth. *Wired* refers to this as "the bite-size bits for high-speed munching." It seems that as our range of attention expands, our depth decreases: We can cast our nets amazingly wide, but not so very deep. But even this limit is the source of a new product opportunity: in 2008, the entertainment component manufacturer JVC introduced the Everio GZ-MS100 with a special upload button that stops filming at the ten-minute mark to obey the YouTube rules; then, it automatically uploads the film to YouTube when it's connected to a PC.

Politics is a great illustration of the yin and yang of user generated content, the enabler and destroyer of careers. Underdog Steve Novick may have lost the Democratic primary for the Senate in Oregon, but by using the YouTube "multiplier effect"—the ability of people you touch on YouTube to touch everyone in their circles—to his advantage he came remarkably close to winning by just 3 percentage points. This was the first time YouTube played a crucial positive role in a statewide race.

The uploading of the George Allen "Macaca" video on YouTube was the "shot heard round the world," but of course, in the other direction. Without the filming by a James Webb operative of Allen's diatribe against him and its subsequent posting to YouTube, it's only a matter of conjecture if Webb could have won the race. It's pretty certain that Allen would have made a serious contender for the Republican nomination for president.

The disintermediation of our political discourse has enabled virtually anyone with a video camera to have a pulpit nearly as "bully" as a network's. We don't rely on television anchor people to explain the news to us; we get it straight from the Internet, focused by the perceptions of a radical range of auteurs who would otherwise not be able to reach us. Robert Greenwald, a film director known for movies like *Xanadu* and

The Burning Bed, produces political spots under the name Brave New Films. "For years, I'd be in conversations with people who said the only way we can be effective is [that] we have to raise $1 billion and buy CBS," he told the *New York Times*. "Well, Google raised a couple of billion and bought YouTube, and it's here for us, and it's a huge difference."[1]

One of his most important spots produced for distribution on YouTube showcased footage of the Reverend Rod Parsley talking about Islam and saying that "America was founded in part with the intention of seeing this false religion destroyed." This was intercut with Senator John McCain admiring comments about the conservative evangelical leader. It didn't take long before the McCain presidential campaign rejected Parsley's endorsement.[2]

What's tremendously crucial here is that Greenwald is not affiliated with any party or campaign. He's a lone operative, funded by the donations of like-minded others. This one and his other videos of McCain that illustrate the senator contradicting himself in a variety of situations had been viewed more than five million times—more than McCain's own promotion films have been played on YouTube—well before the 2008 Republican nominating convention had taken place.

It appears to be becoming ever more of a grassroots trend, with some pundits coining the term "netroots" to monitor the phenomenon. If the Web was initially a great place for campaigns to tell us about themselves and monitor (and edit or delete) our responses, then the Web is where we take back the control with sites such as YouTube and produce our own spots with a hundred dollars' worth of software versus the hundred grand it takes to produce a TV commercial.

The interplay between communicator and recipient gets further blurred as YouTube advances, most recently by offering a free feature to show video creators when and where their videos are being watched. Essentially, this turns the site into "the world's largest focus group," according to Tracy Chan, YouTube product manager.

The idea is that politicians (or rock groups or filmmakers or cereal sellers) can put various messages out on YouTube and see who is watching and when. Then they can craft messages accordingly, tailoring the candidate's speech to appeal in each geography according to how the YouTube video has played there. It is the funhouse mirror effect that Stephen Brown describes and I quoted first at the beginning of chapter 5: "Marketers know about consumers, consumers know about marketers, marketers know consumers know about marketers, consumers know marketers know consumers know about marketers."

"In the future, everyone will be world famous for fifteen minutes," said Andy Warhol famously in 1968—and then had a joke at his own expense by switching the formula around and saying "In the future, fifteen people will be famous." Most likely both things will be true.

The trick of course is that when Warhol was writing there were three national television networks and 200 million people in the United States. Today, there are infinite means of getting our information in front of an audience, but it surely won't be a large one, even though the population has grown by 100 million. Thus, it's both much easier to be famous and much harder: there's more people to reach and more people trying to reach them.

Technology makes it easier for us to find an audience, but it makes the competition for that audience much more aggressive. For example, a Facebook user can have his or her video get its fifteen minutes or longer of excitement, but who knows who they are a week later? An *American Idol* contestant who gets to perform before millions on national television is yesterday's news before the TV set gets turned off. Meanwhile, a few megawatt celebrities continue to dominate.

I'll close with one more personal observation about the passion brand phenomenon: I think we've reached a tipping point in our consumer culture and oddly enough I think it was foretold by Karl Marx when he wrote: "The worker becomes all the poorer the more wealth he produces, the more his production increases in power and range. The worker becomes an ever cheaper commodity the more commodities he creates. . . . Labor produces not only commodities; it produces itself and the worker as a *commodity*—and does so in the proportion in which it produces commodities generally."[3]

I believe that brand passion—a profound emotional connection to certain products with all their symbols and significance—is the antidote we crave to becoming Marxian (or Warholian) commodities ourselves. From the products we genuinely engage with, in all the authentic ways manifest in the examples I've shared, we find a way, albeit a postmodern way, of expressing our individuality, not our commodification. In each conscious choice cobbled together we make a branded pointillist portrait of ourselves and our worldview, one about which we have every right to be passionate.

NOTES

CHAPTER 1

1. Rob Walker, *Buying In: The Secret Dialogue between What We Buy and Who We Are* (New York: Random House, 2008).
2. Pamela L. Alreck and Robert B. Settle, "Strategies for Building Consumer Brand Preference," *Journal of Product & Brand Management* 8, no. 2 (1999): 130–44.

CHAPTER 2

1. Interview with Mandy Ginsberg, June 2008.
2. Interview with Helen Fisher, May 2008.
3. Adam Hanft, "The eHarmony Agenda Gets Called Out on National TV, May 3, 2007, Huffington Post blog.
4. Kevin Lane Keller, *Best Practice Cases in Branding: Lessons from the World's Strongest Brands* (Upper Saddle River, NJ: Pearson Education, 2002), pp. 69–90.
5. Interview with Matthew Gonzalez, April 2005.
6. Richard Florida, *The Rise of the Creative Class* (New York: Basic Books, 2000).

7. Michael Fassnacht, "Postmodern Shopper," Marketing Geek blog, January 28, 2007.

8. Stephen Brown, "Postmodern Marketing: Abutting for Beginners," http://www.sfxbrown.com/Postmodern%20Marketing.pdf (accessed November 30, 2008).

CHAPTER 3

1. Daniel Turner, "The Secret of Apple Design," *Technology Review*, May 2007.

2. Paul Kunkel, *AppleDesign: The Work of the Industrial Design Group* (New York: Watson-Guptill Publications, 1997).

3. Interview with Mark DiMassimo, June 2008.

4. R.Bird & Company, "Research in Package Design for Tea Craze," October 2007.

CHAPTER 4

1. Robert Mondavi with Paul Chutkow, *Harvests of Joy: How the Good Life Became Great Business* (New York: Harcourt and Brace, 1998).

2. Interview with Nina Weims, June 2002.

3. Jean T. Barrett, "The Opus One Winery," *Wine Spectator*, November 15, 1995.

4. Napa/Sonoma author interviews, May 2002.

5. Ibid.

6. Ibid.

7. Ibid.

8. Interview with Gary Heck, October 1980.

9. Interview with Patricia Palermo, November 1997.

10. Napa/Sonoma author interviews, May 2002.

11. From freshdirect.com.

12. Ibid.

13. Author correspondence with Stephen Brown, July 2008.

14. Howard Schultz, *Pour Your Heart Into It: How Starbucks Built a Company One Cup at a Time* (New York: Hyperion, 1997), p. 30.

15. Mark Pendergrast, *Uncommon Grounds: The History of Coffee and How It Transformed Our World* (New York: Basic Books, 1999), p. 292.

16. Cynthia Rosenfeld, "The Aman Way," *Destination*, February/March 2008.

17. Ibid.

18. Nancy F. Koehn, "Howard Schultz and Starbucks Coffee," Harvard Business School case study, November 28, 2001, 9-801-361.

19. Interview with Jerry Noonan, June 2002.

20. Interview with Clotaire Rapaille, January 2005.

21. Koehn, "Howard Schultz and Starbucks Coffee."

22. Ibid.

23. Ibid.

24. Interview with Lori Daniel, June 2008.

25. Roger Yu, "United Flight Canceled after Upset Pilot Refuses to Fly," *USA Today*, June 20, 2008.

26. Millie Olson, "Wanted: More Passion Brands," *Ad Age*, June 17, 2008.

CHAPTER 5

1. Stephen Brown, "O Customer, Where Art Thou?" p. 7.

2. Ibid., p. 4.

3. Ibid., p. 5.

4. Jonathan Bond and Richard Kirshenbaum, *Under the Radar—Talking to Today's Cynical Consumer* (New York: Wiley, 1998), p. 92.

5. William A. Sutton, *Sports Management Quarterly* 6, no. 1.

6. Ibid.

7. George R. Milne and Mark A. McDonald, *Sports Marketing* (Sudbury, MA: Jones and Barlett), p. 13.

8. Daniel Boorstin, *The Americans, the Democratic Experience* (London: Cardinal, 1988), p. 148.

9. Jim McAlexander, John W. Schouten, and Harold F. Koenig, "Building Brand Community," *Journal of Marketing* 66, no. 1 (January 2002): 38–54.

CHAPTER 6

1. Interview with Stephen Brown, June 2008.

2. Penelope Green, "Romancing the Flat Pack: IKEA, Repurposed," *New York Times*, September 6, 2007.

3. David Kiley, "Advertising of, by, and for the People," *Business Week*, July 25, 2005, pp. 63–64.

4. Marketing Society/Opinion Leader, "The Changing Power of Brand in a Brand Democracy," http://www.ol.rarewebs.co.uk/User Files/File/ol/pdf/Marketing%20Society%20Report.pdf (accessed November 26, 2008).

5. Wikipedia, "What Wikipedia Is Not," http://en.wikipedia .org/wiki/Wikipedia_is_not_censored#Wikipedia_is_not_censored (accessed November 24, 2008).

6. Wapedia, "History of Wikipedia," http://wapedia.mobi/en/ History_of_Wikipedia (accessed November 24, 2008).

7. See Threadless.com.

8. Marketing Society/Opinion Leader, "The Changing Power of Brand in a Brand Society."

9. Interview with John Battelle, October 2005.

10. Miguel Helft, "The Humans behind the Google Money Machine," *New York Times*, June 2, 2008.

11. Harris Poll, "Global Pulse US 2008 Study," September 2008.

12. Gary Hamel, *The Future of Management* (Cambridge, MA: Harvard Business Press, 2007), p. 102.

13. Corby Kummer, "Deliverance: The Future of Shopping for Fresh Fruits and Vegetables," *Atlantic*, July/August 2006.

CHAPTER 7

1. Interview with Nahir Patel, February 2006.

2. Stuart Laverick and Kevin Johnston, "The Marketing of a Consumer Icon: Mini Cooper into Japan—Coals to Newcastle?" *Marketing Intelligence & Planning* 15, no. 4 (1997): 179–84.

3. Ibid.

4. Michelle Roehm and Harper Roehm Jr., "Can Brand Encounters Inspire Flashbulb Memories?" *Psychology & Marketing* 24, no. 1 (2007): 25–40.

5. Lynchberg interviews, May 2002.

6. Interview with Cressida Lozano, June 2008.

7. Interview with Richard Wise, June 2008.

8. Interview with Mark Morrissey, June 2008.

9. Maureen Morrin, "The Impact of Brand Extensions on Parent Brand Memory Structures and Retrieval Processes," *Journal of Marketing Research* (November 1999).

10. Interview with Daryl Brewster, April 2008.

11. Rob Walker, "Can Dead Brands Live Again?" *New York Times Magazine*, May 18, 2008.

12. Mike Shine quoted in Michelle Jeffers, "Word on the Street," *Adweek*, May 16, 2005.

13. Stephen Brown, "Sell Me the Old, Old Story," *Journal of Customer Behavior* 2 (2003): 133–47.

14. Chloe Peacock, "Steve Jobs: The Human Logo?" *Networking Knowledge* 1, no. 2 (2007).

15. Leander Kahney, *The Cult of Mac* (San Francisco: No Starch Press, 2004).

CHAPTER 8

1. Interview with Daryl Brewster, June 2008.

2. Joe Nocera, "Put Buyers First: What a Concept," *New York Times*, January 5, 2008.

3. Stephen Brown in correspondence with author.

4. Thane Peterson, "Absolut Michel Roux," *Business Week*, December 4, 2001.

5. Ibid.

6. Interview with Richard Lewis, June 2002.

7. Peterson, "Absolut Michel Roux."

8. Kevin Lane Keller, *Strategic Brand Management*, 2nd ed. (Upper Saddle River, NJ: Prentice Hall, 2003).

9. Kathleen Miller, "Wired: Energy Drinks, Jock Identity, Masculine Norms, and Risk Taking," *Journal of American College Health* 56 (2008): 481–90.

10. Kevin Lane Keller, *Best Practice Cases in Branding: Lessons from the World's Strongest Brands* (Upper Saddle River, NJ: Pearson Education, 2002), pp. 69–90.

11. Tara Parker-Pope, "Taste for Quick Boost Tied to Taste for Risk," *New York Times*, May 27, 2008.

12. Interview with Cressida Lozano and Mark Morrissey, May 2008.

13. Motoko Rich, "Christian Novel Is a Surprise Best Seller," *New York Times*, June 24, 2008.

14. Ibid.

15. Cynthia Rosenfeld, "The Aman Way," *Destination*, February/March 2008.

16. Interview with Mark DiMassimo, June 2008.

17. Michael Solomon, *Conquering Consumerspace: Marketing Strategies for a Branded World* (New York: AMACOM, 2003).

CHAPTER 10

1. Betty Friedan, *The Fountain of Age* (New York: Simon & Shuster, 1994), p. 18.

2. Medline Plus, "Aging Changes in the Senses," *Medical Encyclopedia*, US National Library of Medicine, National Institutes of Health.

CHAPTER 11

1. Robert Putnam, *Bowling Alone: The Collapse and Revival of American Community* (New York: Simon & Schuster, 2000).

2. Naomi S. Baron, Always On: Language in an Online and Mobile World (Oxford: University Press, 2008), p. 223.

3. David Carr, "Taken to a New Place by a TV in the Palm, " *New York Times*, September 15, 2005.

4. "ICR Study of Rudeness in America," 2006 poll conducted for ABC News.

5. Sprint Wireless courtesy report, 2004.

6. Edward Wong, "A Stinging Office Memo Boomerangs; Chief Executive Is Criticized after Upbraiding Workers by E-mail," *New York Times*, April 5, 2001.

7. Andrea Neighbours, "How My Husband Won Back My Vote," *New York Times*, June 22, 2008.

CHAPTER 12

1. Daniel Boorstin, *The Americans, the Democratic Experience* (New York: Vintage Books, 1974), p. 147.

2. Stephen Brown, "Postmodern Marketing," *European Journal of Marketing* 27, no. 4:19–34.

3. Bernard Cova, "The Postmodern Explained to Managers: Implications for Marketing," *Business Horizons* 39, no. 6 (November 1996).

4. Ibid.

CHAPTER 14

1. Jim Rutenberg, "Political Freelancers Use Web to Join the Attack," *New York Times*, June 29, 2008.

2. Ibid.

3. Karl Marx, "Economic and Philosophic Manuscripts of 1844."

ACKNOWLEDGMENTS

First of all, I owe a deep debt to Julie Sheehan, poet, poetry teacher, and writer extraordinaire.

Then, too, the nice folks at Prometheus, editor Steven L. Mitchell, Christine Kramer, Catherine Roberts-Abel, Nicole Lecht, and others who bought the idea of this work and then brought it to the marketplace. And, my agent, Sharlene Martin, who persevered with and for me.

Beyond that, there are many professional colleagues who have engaged on this topic with me, offering up opinions, anecdotes, and perspectives from inside the formation of passion brands: Mandy Ginsberg, Adam Hanft, Helen Fisher, Mark DiMassimo, Doug Shouse, Phyllis Dealy, Mark Morrissey, Richard Wise, Cressida Lozano, Daryl Brewster, Chris Baldwin, Peter Klein, Victor Crain, Peter Connolly, Bob Taraschi, Helen Fitzpatrick, Phil Keen, Vanessa Capobianco, Clare McLeod, Hal Goldberg, Matthew Gonzalez, Norris Bernstein, Richard Lewis, Mike Sinyard, Erik Eidsmo, Jay Cooper, Richard Florida, Missy Park, Nina Weims, and last but by no means least, Faith Popcorn, ever an inspiration.

271

Then, too, I need to say thank you to all the friends I bored to tears with passion brands (and perhaps evangelizing about Fresh Direct too much, too often): John Olsen, Doug Ray, Diane Podrasky, Gary Kaplan, Nancy Smith, John Casey, Serra Yavuz, Joe Sahid, Robin Waxenberg, Isabelle Kellogg, Jayne Sherman, Deby Zum, Barbara Rothberg, Liz Hutchison, Nicole Belmont, and Tim and Kathy Keller.

INDEX